The LEGACY LETTERS

Messages of Life and Hope from 9/11 Family Members

Collected by

Tuesday's Children

Edited by Brian Curtis

A PERIGEE BOOK

A PERIGEE BOOK
Published by the Penguin Group
Penguin Group (USA) Inc.
375 Hudson Street, New York, New York 10014, USA
Penguin Group (Canada), 90 Eglinton Avenue East, Suite 700, Toronto, Ontario M4P 2Y3, Canada
(a division of Pearson Penguin Canada Inc.)
Penguin Books Ltd., 80 Strand, London WC2R 0RL, England
Penguin Group Ireland, 25 St. Stephen's Green, Dublin 2, Ireland (a division of Penguin Books Ltd.)
Penguin Group (Australia), 250 Camberwell Road, Camberwell, Victoria 3124, Australia
(a division of Pearson Australia Group Pty. Ltd.)
Penguin Books India Pvt. Ltd., 11 Community Centre, Panchsheel Park, New Delhi—110 017, India
Penguin Group (NZ), 67 Apollo Drive, Rosedale, Auckland 0632, New Zealand
(a division of Pearson New Zealand Ltd.)
Penguin Books (South Africa) (Pty.) Ltd., 24 Sturdee Avenue, Rosebank, Johannesburg 2196,
South Africa

Penguin Books Ltd., Registered Offices: 80 Strand, London WC2R 0RL, England

While the author has made every effort to provide accurate telephone numbers and Internet addresses at the time of publication, neither the publisher nor the author assumes any responsibility for errors or for changes that occur after publication. Further, the publisher does not have any control over and does not assume any responsibility for author or third-party websites or their content.

First edition: August 2011

Library of Congress Cataloging-in-Publication Data

The legacy letters : messages of life and hope from 9/11 family members / collected by Tuesday's
Children ; edited by Brian Curtis.
    p.   cm.
    ISBN 978-0-399-53708-0
    1. September 11 Terrorist Attacks, 2001—Personal narratives.   2. Terrorism—New York (State)—
New York.   I. Curtis, Brian, 1971–   II. Tuesday's Children.
    HV6432.7.L4384   2011
    974.7'10440922—dc22   2011015553

PRINTED IN THE UNITED STATES OF AMERICA

10   9   8   7   6   5   4   3   2   1

Most Perigee books are available at special quantity discounts for bulk purchases for sales promotions, premiums, fund-raising, or educational use. Special books, or book excerpts, can also be created to fit specific needs. For details, write: Special Markets, Penguin Group (USA) Inc., 375 Hudson Street, New York, New York 10014.

Dedicated to all of the men and women who lost their lives on September 11 and the brave heroes and families left behind.

ACKNOWLEDGMENTS

The Legacy Letters is the result of an incredible team of strangers coming together to create the best book possible. My sincere gratitude and friendship go to Sara Wingerath at Tuesday's Children, who devoted many hours and nights to the project and who never stopped believing in what we were doing. Molly Lieberman was instrumental in working with the families, and Terry Sears gave her full support from the day we began discussing the idea. Tuesday's Children is a remarkable organization for the families of those lost on 9/11.

We couldn't have been more blessed than to have Marian Lizzi create a home for the book at Penguin. Marian's belief in the project, her kind and compassionate approach, and her enthusiasm has set a standard for her fellow editors. Christina Lundy, assistant editor on the project, has gone above and beyond in her duties; Craig Burke, Leslie Schwartz, Jennifer Bernard, Jennifer Eck, Tiffany Estreicher and the entire team at Penguin deserve a thank-you, as does publisher John Duff for having a vision for what this project could be.

On a more personal note, I want to thank my family for their patience. I am a better husband and dad after working on this book.

Most important, I want to thank the family members who opened their hearts to show the world just how much hope and resilience can come from such tragedy. I am inspired and amazed at their attitudes on life, and these new friendships will help guide me forward.

INTRODUCTION

For many of us, particularly those of us in the post-JFK generation, we know when our "Where were you when . . . ?" moment came. I lay asleep in my apartment in Los Angeles, unaware of the tragedy unfolding three thousand miles away in New York, Pennsylvania and Washington. The phone calls started coming in and, like millions of Americans, I was glued to the television for days. I wanted to help, but how? I wanted to fly to New York and volunteer at Ground Zero, but I had no experience or training that would have helped. I wanted to give blood at an L.A. Red Cross but a recent cold prevented that from happening.

As fate would have it, days after the American skies opened again for planes, I found myself blocks from Ground Zero, meeting with a potential publisher for a book project. I took the liberty to walk as close to the site as possible, and from dozens of blocks away, I could see the enormity of the destruction, several stories high.

As anniversaries of September 11 came and went, I was inspired by the stories of the loved ones of the victims, especially the children, and how so many of them managed to turn such a devastating loss into hope in starting foundations, volunteering, following through on their own dreams or, simply, just getting out of bed each morning and living their lives. They were heroes to me. Finally, nine years after September 11, I thought of this small way to help.

Tuesday's Children, an amazing collection of devoted staffers and family members who continue to provide support and programming for the families and the first responders, was the ideal partner for this project. Together, we offered an opportunity for family members to share with us an original letter to their lost loved ones, letters of hope and resiliency. The response was overwhelming and, as you might expect, the task of editing and selecting letters, difficult and emotional. The one hundred letters in this book were selected for a variety of reasons by the editors at Perigee, yet in no way are they any more powerful or important than the many other submissions, the rest of which were published in a keepsake book for the families. Due to space constraints, many of the letters were edited in some manner but all changes were approved by the letter writers.

As you read through these pages, I hope that you will be as inspired by the stories as I have been in working with the families. From resolute mothers to children who never got to hug their parent, the words are heartfelt and honest and should encourage all of us to live our lives with purpose and to cherish every moment. Along with all of those who volunteered at Ground Zero or in Shanksville or at the Pentagon and those who have protected America since September 11, these are the heroes that are the legacy of those lives lost.

Brian Curtis

David Laychak

꧁

David William Laychak was born on January 13, 1961, in Fort Sill, Oklahoma, to Robert and Patricia Laychak. Dave earned a BA from Brown University and an MBA from Syracuse University. After college, he met Laurie Miller while working at the Pentagon and they were married in 1988. They had two children: Zachary in 1992 while living in Syracuse, New York, and Jennifer in 1994 while living in Sierra Vista, Arizona. Dave was a gentle soul who loved his wife, children, church, country and sports. On September 11, Dave was in his office at the Pentagon where he worked as a civilian for the Department of the Army. He was forty years old.

LETTER WRITER: Jennifer Laychak (daughter)
AGE: 16

Dear Dad,

I was seven years old when you were killed. I am now sixteen. I have spent more than half of my life without you. A lot of time has passed, yet those of us who lost someone will never be the same. People think that we have "moved on," but I prefer to think that we have moved forward. Our loss will always be a part of who we are. It is part of our story. As I reread what I wrote in my diary as a little girl, I am amazed at how the thoughts and feelings transcend

time. I still have the same thoughts (although my spelling has improved). I will always miss you.

People focus on the significant moments. You weren't here for my first date, to teach me to drive, or to watch me perform on my school's dance team. You won't be here for my graduation or to walk me down the aisle at my wedding. However, it isn't just the monumental moments that you are missing. It is the small everyday moments. That's what I miss the most. I have to take comfort in knowing that you are within me. I have many of your physical traits that are a part of who I am. I also have some of your character traits as well. Most importantly, I will always carry you in my heart.

Love,
Jenny

JAMES MICHAEL GRAY

≈

James Michael Gray was born on November 8, 1966, in Neptune, New Jersey, to Patrick and Doreen Gray. He married Jean Ferris and had two children, Colleen and Caitlin. He was a firefighter for the New York City Fire Department, Ladder 20 in Soho. He loved spending time with his family and was a fan of the New York Giants. On September 11, James was called to the North Tower. He was thirty-four years old.

LETTER WRITER: **Suzanne Pitzal (sister)**
AGE: **42**

Dear James,

After almost ten years, there is not an hour or day that passes by that I don't think of you.

The respect that we all have for you is so strong. We know how you felt about your job, the fire department, and your "brothers." As a family, we keep that respect for you and all who perished on that day.

In your death, I have lost my only sibling, the only other person in the world that knows how I *really* feel. I've lost the guy who's supposed to be here running around our yard playing ball with my husband, whom you never got to meet, and your children. That is my last memory of you, playing with that big pink rubber ball in the backyard with your girls, Colleen and Caitlin. You were so happy.

In your death, I have gained knowledge of bravery that stuns the world, the legacy of a hero that my daughter is now reading in her history books. I know that when it is my time, you will be there to greet me with open arms. It will be paradise.

Your sister,
Suzanne

MARINA GERTSBERG

~*~

Marina R. Gertsberg was born on February 10, 1976, in the Ukraine to Roman and Anna Gertsberg. She graduated from Binghamton University with a bachelor's degree in Finance and Accounting and was working on a master's degree from Baruch College. She loved music, skiing, swimming, and her family and friends. She worked for Cantor Fitzgerald on the 101st floor of the North Tower. She was twenty-five years old.

LETTER WRITER: Roman Gertsberg (father)
AGE: 61

Dear Marina,
Since September 11, 2001, we have often wanted to see you again, to hug you or to take just one more of our ski trips together—to enjoy just a few more moments with you. But now, we know that you can always be with us, no matter what we do. We keep you in our hearts, so you can be with all of your friends and family all the time.

Many years have passed, and we

5

lost dear family members and we embraced the new born to this world. Your friends already have their own children. These kids see your photo in their homes and know you as Aunt Marina. One of your best friend's twin daughters carries your name as does my nephew's daughter. They will grow to know what a wonderful person you were and what the world lost. You used to call us every day to make sure that we are okay. We miss those calls so much. You were always there for us.

Marina, we hope you can hear us, because we want to say that life-sized dent in our hearts we will fill with love and memories of you and that helps us to move day by day until we meet again. We are proud of you and we want to thank you for the best twenty-five years of our lives. We will treasure your spirit forever.

Your Dad,
Family and Friends

WILLIAM V. STECKMAN

≽€

William V. Steckman was born on December 24, 1944, in New York, New York, to Vincent and Mildred Steckman, and had one sister, Janet. He was married to Barbara and had five children, Donna, Debbie, Deanine, Diana and Billy. He enjoyed boating, family vacations, tinkering around the garage and operating a ham radio, which he was trained to do in the U.S. Coast Guard. He worked at NBC since 1967 where he was a transmitter engineer. On September 11, 2001, he was just finishing up his night shift in a room full of 10,000-watt equipment on the 104th floor of the North Tower, just below the needle. He was fifty-six years old.

LETTER WRITER: Frank DeVito (grandson)
AGE: 15

Dear Pop Pop,
I was five years old on 9/11, too young to understand what really happened. When I found out that you had passed away, I was devastated. You were my favorite person and I would never be able to see you again. Every night I thought about you and all the good times we had together. I even went to a store to get a teddy bear with an angel on him to help keep me happy.

You always taught me to live life to the fullest and enjoy every-

thing that I can. I'll never forget when you promised to take me to your work in the Twin Towers. I loved tugboats, and you wanted to take me there when the tugboats passed by. Now, every year when this tragic day comes around, I relive the good times we had together that I will remember for the rest of my life.

It's hard for someone to say at five years old that someone had an impact on their life, but you had a huge impact on mine. Some of the positive things I learned from you are to live life in happiness no matter what happens and to choose the way you live your life—never let anyone tell you that you can't.

I will always cherish the great five years I knew you, and I am lucky to say that you are my Grandpa.

Forever missing you,
Frankie

VINCENT DIFAZIO

Vincent F. DiFazio was born on May 21, 1958, in New York, New York, to Vincent and Fran DiFazio, and was the brother of Sal, Teresa and Grace. He met his wife, Pattie Toohey, at Glassboro State University, and the two were married in 1984. They had three children, Joe, Gina and Dana. His family was the only thing he loved more than his Yankees, Giants, Knicks and Rangers, and he's remembered for his unique ability to connect with people from all walks of life and to find ways to make them smile. Vincent was a stockbroker at Cantor Fitzgerald, and he was at his desk on the 105th floor of the North Tower on September 11. He was forty-three years old.

LETTER WRITER: Joe DiFazio (son)
AGE: 23

Dad,

I guess it makes the most sense to start at the end.

The last time I saw you, you had a triple stack of powdered donuts piled on top of a belly that looked used to that sort of thing. Confectioner's sugar dusted your lips, and every time the Giants' defense missed a tackle, you pounded a chubby fist into the couch and left a phantom smudge. You were barely five-ten, bald and out of shape.

I looked at you and saw the strongest man in the world.

"All right, time for bed," you said. It was only the third quarter and I turned my head to argue, but you knew what was coming.

"I don't want to hear it," you told me. "It's your first week of high school and you're gonna start it off strong."

I stalked off, headed for the stairs leading to my room. No hug, no kiss goodnight.

I grumbled under my breath. *It's not fair. This sucks.*

"I love you, champ," you told the back of my head. You knew I was pissed, and you weren't really expecting an answer. You didn't get one.

I never heard your voice again.

Well, old man, it's been ten years since you stuffed those donuts down your throat. I'm six foot three, 185 pounds. I'm a Boston College graduate, but don't worry . . . those Sox fans didn't infect me with their nonsense. When I grabbed hold of my diploma I could almost feel you up on that stage next to me. Wherever you were, I know you were smiling.

I've been to music festivals, rode a motorcycle, and gambled in Atlantic City.

I've been in love. I've been heartbroken.

I've missed you every day.

Remember when you took me to that World Series game, when Tino hit the grand slam even though he took strike three the pitch before and the ump bailed him out? I watched the ball sail into those right-field seats and felt the roar of that crowd force the air up out of my lungs. Every pair of eyes in the stadium stared at the field, but when I looked up at you, I saw that you were looking right back at me, more interested in observing your son's joy than you were in the game. Afterward, we sat in traffic for hours on the Bronx streets, and you turned on the Stones and strummed the air guitar, then put a hand on my shoulder. I've never felt safer in my life.

I wish that someday you could have held *my* kids. I wish I could stand and watch from the bedroom doorway while you sat beside them and sang about the young cowboy who lives on the range. I know the words—I'll do my best.

I've spent hours lying in bed, staring at the ceiling, talking to your memory in the dark. I ask for help when I'm confused, for strength when I'm scared, and for comfort when I'm upset. I wonder how it was just at the end—if you were afraid . . . if there was pain.

You never answer, and that's okay.

But more than anything, I wish I could hear your voice again, even just for a minute. I wish I could listen to your stories and to the laugh that lit the room. I wish I could hear you tell me that you're proud.

I need you to know how thankful I am for *everything*.

Thank you for teaching me to hold my head high, to be confident in who I am and in what I do, and to stand up for those who can't stand up for themselves.

Thank you for teaching me how to hit a curveball, to make a free throw and to run a sharp slant.

Thank you for showing me that laughter can cure all, but that it's okay to cry.

Thank you for showing me how to be a man.

I'll always remember to look out for Mom and my little sisters, to treat women like the angels they are and to show kindness to everyone, *especially* those who need it most.

I'll always remember that the guy who sees it the longest hits it the best.

I love you too, Dad, and I'll miss you forever.

Your son,
Joe

Uhuru Gonja Houston

Uhuru Gonja Houston, known as Bee, was born on August 22, 1969, in Brooklyn, New York, to Ian and Estella Crandon, and was the brother of Kyra, Efia and Anane. Bee attended Norfolk State University where he majored in Computer Science. Bee returned to New York where he became a police officer with the Port Authority of New York and New Jersey in 1993. He married his college sweetheart, Sonya Hudley, in 1996 and had two children, Hasani and Hannah. Bee had a contagious smile and loved spending time with his family. He was also creative and ambitious, and a huge Giants fan. On September 11, Bee was working in the North Tower on a plainclothes detail. He was thirty-two years old.

LETTER WRITER: Sonya Houston (wife)
AGE: 41

Dear Bee,

Yet another gorgeous early fall day, with the temps in the high 70s to low 80s, warm, only a few fluffy cumulus clouds in the sky. The perfect day to be outside . . .

Ten years earlier, the weather was the same. The day our lives would change forever.

By now, we all know the events of that horrific day that would change America and my life forever. No need to go all the way back right now.

Uhuru, Hasani, Hannah and Sonya

I want to fast-forward you to the page we are on now. The book that is still being written, the lives that are still being lived and the pain that still exists. This is just a reality check of a life that was changed in a blink of an eye. An angel that was taken too soon and his legacy that must continue on through his children.

People ask us, "How are you doing?" with that sad, head-tilted-to-the-side, and somber look of pain and anguish.

"We are good," I respond, with the same tilt, and somber smile that holds a lot of pain. "The kids are fine, getting big. Hasani is in his first year of high school now; Hannah is in the fifth grade and enjoys doing flips and is a social butterfly. And the baby, Haven, who is almost three years old. Wow, time sure does move quickly."

They usually continue on and I go about my life. This new, re-built life minus you, my beloved husband.

You were a great man, with a contagious smile that lit up the room as soon as you walked in. Everyone loved you. You were a man who truly came into his own, a wonderful, creative, funny man who loved his family. You were a great provider and as sweet as sweet potato pie that you enjoyed eating at Thanksgiving. I can't sing the praises of you enough. Not enough words in the English dictionary to describe you and do you justice, so I will stop here.

So with three children now and living in New York City, there is always something going on. Needless to say, my life is always moving and shaking. The kids keep me extremely busy and their schedules are crazy. They have auditions, basketball, dance, tutoring, music class and education, which is still so high on our list of priorities. Studying and homework becomes a huge part of our day.

You never know where your help will come from. We take it as it comes. I've learned to not question things—why and where "help" comes from. Just take it. We have learned to be very independent and do things on our own, so to accept help can be difficult at times.

Mom is your biggest cheerleader. She always wears her PAPD T-shirts, and with the same tilted head and somber look explains to EVERYONE how she lost her son on 9/11. She tells her friends in Maryland, "You know, I gotta go to New York 'cause of 9/11." She almost brags about it. Not in a gloating way but because she really misses you. I try not to let everyone know. She does the opposite. I believe this is her way of dealing with her grief as well. She is so strong.

The children keep me young, and they remind me every day of you. You live on through them. Hasani's disposition and mannerisms are all you. Hannah looks like you but is very feminine and girly. They both are kind and compassionate children. I can't wait to see who they become as they grow up. I know you are looking down on them and smiling. You would be so proud.

Love always
and forever,
Sonya

Derek Statkevicus

꽃

Derek James Statkevicus was born on May 26, 1971, in Endicott, New York, to Joseph and Nancy Statkevicus, and was the brother of Joel. Derek earned his BS in Accounting from Ithaca College and worked as a research analyst for Keefe, Bruyette & Woods. Derek married Kimberly Young in 1998 and had two children, Tyler in August 2000 and Derek "Chase" in January 2002. Derek loved his family, his dog Squirt and the New York Yankees. On September 11, Derek was at his desk on the 89th floor of the South Tower. He was thirty years old.

LETTER WRITER: Derek "Chase" Statkevicus (son)
AGE: 9

Dear Daddy Derek,
I wish I could have met you. It makes me sad that I don't even have a picture of the two of us together. Someday I'll see you in heaven. I love you so much.

Love,
Chase

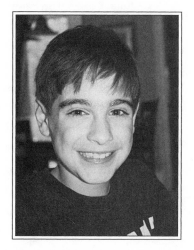

CARL BEDIGIAN

Carl John Bedigian was born on August 31, 1966, in Queens, New York, to Joseph and Dolores Bedigian, and was the brother of Joseph Jr. and Robert. He married Michele Becker in 2000. Carl was a New York City firefighter who spent most of his FDNY career in Engine 214 in Bedford-Stuyvesant, Brooklyn. He was a romantic who loved to cook, build homes and collect motion Hallmark ornaments. He had a smile that could truly melt your heart. On September 11, Carl was one of five members from his firehouse who never returned home. He was thirty-five years old.

LETTER WRITER: Michele Bedigian (wife)
AGE: 40

Dear Carl,

It's been almost ten years since your death, and in that time, I've worked so hard at trying to understand what has happened to the life I dreamt of as a little girl.

That vision is gone now, but through so much darkness, there are these glimmers of clarity of what life really means that I never would have seen had 9/11 not happened.

The gratitude I carry is for the life I had with you, and for all of the unexpected that I've experienced since then.

It's for the blessed relationships I've made with other women who, too, wear my shoes.

It's for the outpouring of love and support I've received from total strangers over the years.

It's for the chance to help another in a meaningful way, by just being there and "knowing the feeling" or having the chance to help them find peace somewhere in this world.

My good friend Sarah said that I've always had a choice on how I reacted to losing you. She said that although my life will never have the picture-perfect story I dreamt of as a little girl, it is still mine to live.

From the moment you perished, each obstacle has taught me something more about myself, and about the potential every one of us is capable of. Consequently I uncovered a truth, that happiness is a choice, one that takes courage and a genuine commitment.

I still want a family, I want to be a mother, I want to love and be loved. I want to have someone to grow old with in this lifetime.

When I remarried in October of 2006, the decision to say "yes" did not come easily. There were feelings of disloyalty, guilt and even fear that I was hurting you. But the choice was mine to make, and I felt blessed to have found another opportunity at happiness. So many times I wasn't sure I could take a step. But I did (with faith) and somehow found the courage to be open to love again. Walking down the aisle symbolized this great bridge between past and future.

I'm thinking about the dream I had of you about a month ago. Maybe it was a visit?

Nonetheless what you said was a gift I'll treasure forever:

You and I are the same spark. So your life is my life. Your children are my children. You've fulfilled us by having the strength to go forward. The future is beautiful and I'm right here with you. Go make a life for us all. Choose happy and I love you.

Your philosophy was simple—in order to be all things possible, one must try.

It took me nine years to discover that it's okay to laugh again, and it's more than okay to try.

I promise.

Thank you, my love.

Always,
Michele

JIMMY STRAINE

James "Jimmy" Joseph Straine Jr. was born on February 5, 1965, in Lawton, Oklahoma, to James and Mary Straine, and was the brother of Michael, Kathleen, Kevin and Daniel. He married Patricia Carr in 1993 and had two children, Finn and Charles. Jimmy earned a BA from East Carolina University and worked as a repurchase agreements salesman for Cantor Fitzgerald. He loved his children and wife, ECU football, golf, playing pickup basketball, fishing, telling stories and spending time with family and friends. On September 11, Jimmy was at his desk on the 104th floor of the North Tower. He was thirty-six years old.

LETTER WRITER: Michael Straine (brother)
AGE: 45

Dear Jimmy,

I still cannot believe it will be ten years since that tragic day.

It started out like many others. It was a beautiful late summer day. The sky was as clear and the air as crisp as you will ever see. I was at my desk on the trading floor at Credit Suisse First Boston on 24th Street in Manhattan when my boss emerged from his office and notified us that some sort of prop plane had hit the WTC. A few minutes later, we saw the first pictures on the trading floor televisions. Once I saw that black smoke billowing from the top floors, I knew that this was not a prop plane. I immediately thought of you and your pals on the 104th floor of 1 World Trade.

They never recovered any of your remains, nor any of your co-workers. I know that you were together until the end and that you, ever the eternal optimist, kept them feeling safe and full of hope.

Jimmy, I just want to let you know that ten years later not a day goes by that we don't think about you. As time has passed the memories have become much less painful as our hearts fill with joy at the mere mention of your name. There are lots of new people in our lives and every one of them has come to know you through the stories we tell and by looking at your two little boys who are growing into fine young men. (And great little point guards.)

Mom and Dad are doing great. Playing lots of golf and enjoying life down in Haig Point.

Jimmy (left) and Michael

Dugan James and I are doing well, and I am sure that you would love Colleen. Dugan and I take our annual trip to the 9/11 Memorial in the Highlands, and he continually asks me to tell him stories about "you and Uncle Jimmy when you were my age."

Danny got married to Erin last summer. Your old surfboard stood in for you during the ceremony. It was classic!

And finally, Trisha, Stuart, Finn, Charlie, Declan and Adele are a wonderful family. I am sure that you are looking down on them in comfort and joy when you see the beautiful, loving family that they have become. Katy and Bernie now have three as Patrick James has joined Quinn and Ryan in the O'Hara family. Kevin and Erin have three as well. Hugh and Duncan are molded straight from *The Little Rascals*, while Ennis is the cutest little girl you have ever seen.

Miss you, bro!

Love,
Mike

Dennis Michael Edwards

Dennis Michael Edwards was born on April 28, 1966, in Huntington, New York, to Morgan and Julia Edwards, and was the brother of Sheila, Morgan, Lisa and Eileen. He married Patti Kavanaugh in 1996 and had a daughter, Alexa, now twelve. He loved spending time with his wife and daughter. He was always working on their house and yard. He loved hanging out with and helping family and friends. Dennis worked for Cantor Fitzgerald. He was at his desk on September 11 on the 105th floor of the North Tower. He was thirty-five years old.

LETTER WRITER: Brooke Cortese (niece)
AGE: 19

Dear Dennis,

Not a day goes by that I don't look at the picture of the two of us from when I was a baby. You were throwing me up into the air and all I could do was laugh. You were my first Valentine and always will be. I have so many memories with you that I remember every single day.

I wish we could have had more time together to make more memories. My only other wish is that you are proud of the young woman that I have become.

I promise not to be too sad when I think of you, and I promise to remember all the happy times we had together, because just to have known you for those few short years has been a gift that I will always cherish. I promise to laugh as much as I can, like I know you would have wanted.

I love you so much. Please keep an eye on us from heaven.

Love,
Brooke

STEPHEN KEVIN TOMPSETT

❧

Stephen Kevin Tompsett was born on January 27, 1962, in Sydney, Australia, to Jack and Rae Tompsett, and was the brother of Geoffrey, Elizabeth and Ian. Stephen earned his degree from the University of Sydney. In 1986, he came to New York with an Australian firm on a project for which his future wife, Dorry, worked. They were married on September 30, 1989, and their daughter, Emily, was born on September 22, 1991. In 1992, Stephen was hired by Instinet Corporation, where he quickly rose to Senior Vice President of Corporate Technology. Stephen dearly loved and was devoted to his family, was proud to be Australian and a New Yorker, and was passionate about golf and all things technological. On September 11, 2001, he was attending a conference at Windows on the World in the North Tower. He was thirty-nine years old.

LETTER WRITER: Dorry Tompsett (wife)
AGE: 46

My Dearest Love:
There are so many things you have missed . . . big events like Em's graduation from grade school, her first play in high school, her first boyfriend and Sweet Sixteen party, her valedictorian speech at high school graduation and moving her to college. You missed the hard

times too, especially Marty's illness and death. I know you welcomed him into heaven but we all needed you here with your quiet
strength.

I miss you in the little things so much as well . . . holding my
hand at the Our Father at Mass . . . saying, "Hello, my girls!" in
your beautiful voice with your lovely Aussie accent . . . sleeping in
on Sundays . . . knowing that you were always there to help, protect
and love us.

Every time some new technology is released it hurts me and I
miss you even more . . . so many things you would have loved. Cell
phones access the Internet and get emails now, and texting has
become the way young people communicate.

How many times I ached that you weren't here to talk to Em
about math. I know you know that she was the top math student
in high school and that she's found Computer Science in college as

well. She is going to be a Computer Science teaching assistant this year, and I know you are proud that she wants to teach math . . . I so wish she could talk to you!

We still talk to your mum and dad every week, and we've visited the family almost every year. We talk about you and feel your presence here and in Oz.

I know you are watching us from heaven, putting your angel wings around all of us. But how I wish you were here! If I close my eyes I can feel you standing next to me, letting me lean against you, hearing your beautiful soft voice saying, "I love you, my honey."

All my love always,
D

STAN SMAGALA

~᚛~

Stanley Smagala Jr. was born on April 6, 1965, in Bayshore, New York, to Stanley Sr. and Florence Smagala, and was the youngest of seven children. He grew up and lived his whole life on Long Island. He joined the New York City Fire Department in 1996. He was married to his wife, Dena, for three years, and they were expecting their first child, Alexa. Some of Stan's hobbies included golf, softball and Ping Pong, as well as being a Mets and Jets fan. He was thirty-six years old.

LETTER WRITER: Jim Smagala (brother)
AGE: 47

Dear Stan,

I am so proud of you.

You were a New York City firefighter stationed at Engine 226 in Brooklyn who traveled across the Brooklyn Bridge with your company that fateful day to perform the duties that you swore an oath to uphold. I, too, took that solemn oath. I traveled across that same bridge, that same day, to carry out my duties as a New York City firefighter. I made it back home. You did not. You left your family, your wife, your unborn child behind. Truly tragic.

Through tragedy, though, come important lessons to be learned, hard as they may be.

Jim (left) and Stan

You and I were the best of friends. We worked together, played softball together, grew to be young men together. We argued at times. We had feelings of bitterness and jealousy. I don't regret those feelings. We were still great friends.

One thing I do regret, though, is taking our relationship for granted. Not having the foresight to see that it would not last forever. I just expected that it would. We always had each other, you and I. Most of our seven brothers and sisters had moved out while we were in our early teens, so we spent a great deal of time together. I expected that we would be there for each other, till the end. We would raise our kids together, take our families on vacations together, grow old together. That all changed on September 11, 2001. A date that I can't even stand to hear mentioned anymore. Reality set in that day and woke me up to the fact that nothing is forever in this world. The things we so easily take for granted can be taken from us in an instant, even though we fool ourselves into believing that they won't. They were taken from us suddenly and without warning when you were just thirty-six years old.

I've since retired from the fire department. My time there is just a memory now. I've learned not to take relationships for granted anymore. I cherish the time I spend with my wife, my kids, our mother, brothers and sister with the same fervor that I wished I had done with you when you were with us. I will not make that mistake again. I know now how easily it can all be swept away.

In reading newspaper articles, watching the news on TV and from talking to people I know, I often hear stories about family rifts, arguments or tragedies leaving families at odds with each other. I think how sad it is that they have not learned the important lesson that I have learned.

Stan, I love you and I miss our time together.

Your brother,
Jim

Hagay Shefi

🌿

Hagay Shefi was born on October 24, 1966, in Tel Aviv, Israel, to Dov and Esther Shefi, and was the brother of Yishai and Pazit. He was President and CEO of GoldTier Tech with a background in global execution and management of high-tech companies. Hagay was a keynote speaker at many industry conferences worldwide. On September 11, 2001, he was serving as keynote speaker in a conference for directors of banks, assembled on behalf of Risk Waters Group at Windows on the World in the North Tower. He was thirty-four years old.

LETTER WRITER: Dov Shefi (father)
AGE: 78

Dear Hagay,

On 9/11/01, your mother and I were at home, in a suburb of Tel Aviv, Israel. The news broadcast was opened with a description that "a small airplane crashed into one of the WTC Towers." After two seconds, our TV was turned to CNN. We watched a big passenger airplane crash into the South Tower of WTC. Your mother started to worry and suggested that we call you and Sigal. I tried to convince her that there was nothing to worry about, since your business was located in New Jersey.

Mother refused to agree (Mother is always a mother), so I tried to get you by phone. There was only a taped answer with your voice.

Your mother insisted that we call your wife from Israel. Sigal's phone was occupied ten minutes but finally she answered and said, "Yes, Hagay is there at WTC, 106th floor. He was invited to speak as a keynote speaker at a Conference of Directors of Banks at Windows on the World on the 106th floor of the North Tower." Sigal told us that you called her and said that a bomb had exploded and there is a lot of smoke in the building. You added that you did not believe that the people on the floor would survive and you used farewell words.

We shall never forget the moment that we heard the news. We felt that the heavens fell on us.

We cannot believe that you will not be with us physically. However, your memory will be preserved by everyone in our family. You have been a most loyal son, husband to Sigal, and father to Roy, fifteen, and Naomi, thirteen. You were loved and appreciated by your brother, Yishai, and your sister, Pazit, and their families. All your friends in the United States and in Israel miss your loyal friendship and your sense of humor. It has been said that you were the heart and the dynamo-buster-turbo of every company you were running. All of us in the family will remember you forever and you will continue to be in our hearts and our source of pride. We shall provide Sigal and your kids—our beloved grandchildren, Roy and Naomi—the best of our love and care. Rest in peace.

Love,
Dad

MICHAEL EDWARD McHUGH JR.

꿍

Michael Edward McHugh Jr. was born on March 9, 1966, in Bronx, New York, to Michael McHugh Sr. and Eileen Higgins, and was the brother of John and Darby. He married Maria Cermele in 1993 and had three children, Michael III, Christian and Connor. Michael earned his BA from Iona College; worked for TradeSpark, a subsidiary of Cantor Fitzgerald; and held an elected position as Tuckahoe Village Trustee. He loved playing with his sons and spending time with his wife and family. On September 11, Michael was at his desk on the 101st floor of the South Tower. He was thirty-five years old.

LETTER WRITER: Maria McHugh (wife)
AGE: 43

Dear Michael,

Let me begin by saying how much we all miss you. There is not a day that goes by that we do not think of you; however, we are constantly reminded of your spirit because it is obvious in your sons' faces.

We are all well but definitely a little broken. The days following your passing were filled with incredible disbelief. Nobody really could grasp what was truly happening—in the world around us and in the comfort of our home. It took a few days to realize you would not come home and that our lives would never be the same. The feeling of your loss was devastating.

Your family is well but your brother John's sudden passing just a couple of years ago brought a deep sadness, again, to their hearts and souls. His death, like yours, was quick and without goodbyes. Your family is remarkable to have gone through so much pain and yet continues to give with all of their hearts.

From the beginning, I decided to raise the boys with you in mind every step of the way, hoping to keep our values alive in their everyday. I wanted them to feel secure and loved, and knowing that gave me the focus and the strength I needed to try to make the best choices for them. To say that you would be proud of the individuals Michael, Christian and Connor have become is an understatement. There is something McHugh in each of their faces and personalities. And although they only knew you for a moment in time, you will never be forgotten. We speak of you freely and pray for you often. They are so beautiful and smart and funny, and I cannot thank you enough for giving me a most incredible family.

I tormented myself for a long time for missing your phone call that dreadful morning. I don't know if you called to say I love you, take care of my boys and please make sure they remember me, or just goodbye, but that's what I imagine now. I'm so sorry I wasn't there for you in your darkest moment. I will never forgive myself for that.

I played the anniversary present you gave me the week before over and over again. "I Hope You Dance" could be heard morning, noon and night, but never enough. It was the simplest and most significant gift you had ever given me, but you probably already knew that.

I have followed your advice and danced, trying to live with purpose and without regret. I have since remarried and now Michael, Christian and Connor have a new baby brother, Anthony. He is remarkable and I can't picture our lives without him. Our struggles are the same these days as we are all striving for that happy place.

Thank you for giving me the best part of you. I will always love you.

Maria

Mark Lawrence Charette

🕊

Mark Lawrence Charette was born on February 19, 1963, in Warwick, Rhode Island, to Lawrence and Donnalee Charette, and was the brother of Gregory. A former lieutenant in the U.S. Navy, he graduated with a bachelor's degree from the University of Pennsylvania's Wharton School. There he met his wife, Cheryl Desmarais. They had three children, Lauren, Andrew and Jonathan (ages eight, six and one on September 11, 2001). Mark was an incredible father and man of integrity who somehow managed to spend an enormous amount of time with his family. He loved woodworking, golfing, skiing, and hiking and camping with his family. Mark was a Senior Vice President at Marsh & McLennan. Though his office was in New Jersey, on September 11 he was holding annual planning meetings for his group on the 100th floor of the North Tower. He was thirty-eight years old.

LETTER WRITER: Lauren Charette (daughter)
AGE: 18

Dad,

Could you answer some of the questions I'll never get to ask? I'm looking at colleges—which one should I pick?

I passed my black belt test like I promised. Were you watching? Did you see me spar at nationals?

I'm graduating in June. Will you clap for me?

I passed my driver's test—isn't that scary?

Did you know that Jonathan has the same color eyes as yours?

I don't remember what I wanted to be when I was little. Do you remember?

Have you seen my drawings? Haven't they come a long way from the stick figures I used to draw?

Do you think I've made good friends?

Are you proud of my grades?

I'm playing volleyball and I play setter. That's what you played, right?

Andrew, Mark, Jonathan and Lauren

I finally found the waterfall we used to hike to—remember that?

I still haven't beat our distance record for sledding. Think I'll manage it this year?

I skied the Black Hole—did you see me?

I still can't spell—would you quiz me?

I've read almost all the books you have. Did you like them as much as I did?

I stopped going to church. Does it matter?

When you get this will you write back?

I saw *Quest for Camelot* again. Isn't it the greatest movie ever?

Do you miss me as much as I miss you?

Will you be at my wedding?

Do you think I'm picking the right career?

Do you miss going out to breakfast?

Did you know I learned how to start a campfire?

I still can't catch any fish—funny, huh?

Would you still take my door off the hinges when I slam it?

Hey, Dad, why's the sky blue?

I've forgotten. What's your favorite color?

Do you remember the beach? Could you teach me how to build sandcastles?

Have you read what I wrote?

Would you go hiking with me?

Do you love me?

Most of all I wanted to ask, am I still your little girl?

Forever,
Lauren

HOWARD LEE KANE

~

Howard Lee Kane was born on May 6, 1961, in Queens, New York, to Bruce and Rochelle Kane, and was the brother of Holly and Adam. He wed Lori Renz in 1989 and had a son, Jason, in 1990. He earned a bachelor's degree in Accounting from Pennsylvania State University. Howard worked as comptroller for prestigious New York restaurants such as the Rainbow Room and, most recently, Windows on the World. His passions included cooking, fishing, gardening and spending time with his family. On September 11, Howard was at work on the 107th floor of the North Tower. He was forty years old.

LETTER WRITER: Jason Kane (son)
AGE: 20

Dear Dad,

Although I was only eleven years old on that fateful day, you still remain a vivid memory in my mind and a bold impression on my heart. Some may say that ten years is too long a time to recollect memories for someone who was so young at the time, but I disagree. I have lucid memories of the father you are for me. I remember you would leave the house long before I would wake for school, to take New Jersey Transit and the Path train to the towers, and you

would return home between 8:00 p.m. and midnight on weekdays. The weekends you dedicated to Mom and me. I remember going on daytrips, playing video games, swimming, enjoying pancake breakfasts, fishing with you—just to name a few things. You taught me how to be fair and how to be a good person from the short time we had together.

I also know you through the memories of others. My mother, grandparents, aunts, uncles and cousins tell me about your sense of humor and your seemingly limitless kindness. You always put others' needs ahead of your own.

Continuing my college years, some may say I am finding my own independence, learning how to live life on my own. As I evolve, I realize that most of my life lessons come from you. When I need a reminder of how to act or what to do, I think of you. Spiritually, I will never be alone. I am always striving to reach the standards that you set for me.

Thank you for the inspiration you continue to give me each day.

Love, your son,
Jason

Anthony Mark Ventura

Anthony Mark Ventura was born on June 12, 1960, in Brooklyn, New York, to Dominic and Margaret Ventura, and had two brothers, Louis and Christopher. Anthony received his bachelor's degree from New York University. He married Lisa on June 11, 1994, and had two daughters, Jessica and Nicole. Besides being a devoted father and husband, Anthony was an avid bike rider and reader. He also had a love for automobiles—spending most of his free time cruising the lots of nearby dealerships. He was a Senior Vice President at Fiduciary Trust Company, which was located in the South Tower. He was forty-one years old.

LETTER WRITER: Lisa Ventura (wife)
AGE: 46

Dear Anthony,
It is so hard to believe that ten years have passed, because in some ways, the heartache feels like yesterday, and in others, I can't believe that we as a family survived your absence.

There are many things that bring me joy throughout the year. I smile each time I think about us cutting down and decorating our Christmas tree. You knew how important that was for me, since I never did that as a child. You were all about family, declaring weekends as family time. Only you would take a twenty-mile bike ride at 7:00 a.m. so that you could be home and ready to start your day with your family. We knew we came first—thank you!

You would be so proud of the girls and who they are today. They are so much like you. Jessica loves to read. She always has a book in her hand. Nicole is my handyman—always putting things together or taking things apart. That was so you.

One of the things that I admired most about you was your love for my mother, Felicia. She was welcomed into our home and into our lives. It is no wonder that she loved you the way she did. I was happy knowing that you and she were working for the same company. And it is no wonder that you sacrificed your safety to go and get my mother on that tragic day. I knew when I was told that you were last seen going up the stairwell that you were on your way to get my mom. I knew that was never a choice but a given. Losing both of you on September 11 was beyond pain, but knowing that you were together when your lives ended brought me some source of comfort.

Life is different from how I envisioned it nineteen years ago. So much has changed but we managed to carve out a blessed life. You were, and continue to be, a source of hope, inspiration and love. I am thankful that God gave us the time that we had. You will continue to live in our hearts, souls and minds. We will always love you and pray that you and Mom are in peace and watching over us as we live this life that God has decided us to live.

Love,
Lisa

Felicia Hamilton

ᕁᕁ

Felicia Hamilton was born on June 20, 1939, in Nusco, Italy, to Rosalie and Pasquale Mongelluzzo, and was the sister of Antonio, Maria and Rachel. She married Walter Hamilton and had two children, Walter Jr. and Lisa. She worked for Fiduciary Trust. She loved her children, daughter-in-law Donna, son-in-law Anthony (see previous letter), grandchildren Jessica and Nicole, and the New York Mets and Rangers, and she was an excellent cook. On September 11, Felicia was at her desk on the 97th floor of the South Tower. She was sixty-two years old.

LETTER WRITER: **Walter Hamilton (son)**
AGE: **47**

Dear Mom,

When G-d made you, the mold was broken. You were a woman who put her children, family and friends first—many times to her detriment. I remember how you always found time to take us and many of our friends to ballgames, parks and museums, even while you had to work nights to support us.

When we were children, you were our role model, provider and someone we tried to please.

When we became adults, you were our best friend, confidante and someone who always put our needs and concerns first.

I remember you sitting through my Little League baseball games and my sister's dance recitals. You seemed like you were watching the best in the world for hours at a time, just by watching your children enjoy themselves.

You read to us every night and taught us the importance of reading. How you were able to do this while working nights and raising two kids still amazes me.

You taught us the value of money and the importance of saving, and in these times, that is one of the most important lessons I have learned. Much of this was ingrained in you by being born and raised poor on a farm in Italy during World War II.

I believe that Hallmark must have based their Mother's Day cards on you. For some, these are just words. For you, it was your way of life.

You were a devout Catholic. When we were children, every Saturday evening we would accompany you to service at St. Mary's Church. I always remember you praying the Rosary and carrying the rosary. I gave you a beautiful rosary that was with you on 9/11/01. I hope it helped you through it. Your beliefs and faith have found their way into me and have given me strength through these dark times. In heaven, I know you have found your rightful place with the saints.

Love always,
Walter

BILLY DEAN

~

William "Billy" Dean was born on February 8, 1966, in New York, New York, to Malcolm and Eleanor Dean, and was the middle child between siblings Mark, Beverly, Malcolm Jr., Donna and Timothy. He married Patricia McGovern in 1994 and had one child, Matthew, and was expecting his second child, Claire, in December of 2001. Billy received his BA from the College of Insurance. He enjoyed all sports but was most passionate about basketball, golf and running, even completing the NYC marathon and several sprint triathlons. He loved playing with Matthew and was thrilled about having another child. He was a Vice President at Marsh & McLennan on the 100th floor of the North Tower. His location on September 11 is unknown. He was thirty-five years old.

LETTER WRITER: Claire Dean (daughter)
AGE: 9

Dear Daddy,
You died on 9/11. I wasn't born yet so I never met you, but I know some things about you. You were funny and smart. You were athletic and a good cook. You loved to travel to different places and be upstate at your family's summer house. Mom told me that you used

to talk to me while I was inside her belly. You were only thirty-five years old when you died. I have an older brother, Matthew, who was only three years old when you died, so he really didn't know what was happening. Matthew is an athlete like you.

Every year we have a party for you to remember you. It's called "Billy Dean Day." My whole family misses you, but we know you are watching over us. Sometimes I see you in my dreams as a beautiful angel watching over me and my family because you love us and always will love us.

Love,
Claire

MICHAEL FRANCIS LYNCH

Michael Francis Lynch was born on May 6, 1968, in Flushing, New York, to Daniel and Catherine Lynch, and was the youngest of eight: Kathleen, Bernadette, Mary, Rory, Barbara, Danny and Maureen. He married Denise Bertrand in 1997 and had two sons, Michael and Jack. Michael graduated from SUNY Albany in 1990. He joined the New York City Fire Department in 1991 and spent ten years assigned to Ladder 4 in Midtown Manhattan. Michael was studying for the Lieutenant's test. He loved his wife and children; the New York Mets, Jets and Knicks; playing basketball and reading. On September 11, Michael was one of fifteen firefighters from his firehouse (Ladder 4, Engine 54, Battalion 9) lost rescuing people from the South Tower. After 9/11, Michael was posthumously promoted to Lieutenant by the FDNY. He was thirty-three years old.

LETTER WRITER: Bernadette Lynch Rafferty (sister)
AGE: 54

Dear Mike,

You died in the line of duty, rescuing civilians trapped in an elevator at the World Trade Center. It was the second tower hit by a plane and the first to go down. They found your body six months and one day later. It was intact, with the jaws of life lying next to you.

A woman came to the firehouse and spoke on how the Ladder 4 firefighters rescued her after she had fallen into the elevator shaft. The Ladder 4 firefighters pulled her to safety with a human chain. She lived, and they placed her in an ambulance. Then the building collapsed.

You are a true hero along with the fifteen firefighters from your house who perished.

Mike, I guess you know that our sister Maureen died ten months after you of breast cancer. After 9/11 and Maureen's death, it was very difficult for our family, but people helped us by just

listening and being there for us. I moved forward after 9/11. The human spirit has strength and there is no other alternative but to go on.

We miss you every time we look at your boys, Jack and Michael. Jack is now ten and Michael will be thirteen. They are beautiful and great basketball players. Denise is still healing and so are we.

Up the block from our grammar school, the street is named after you: Firefighter Michael Francis Lynch Way. Every September, we have a golf outing at Mary's country club. We honor you and Maureen on that day. We have given out many scholarships for children from St. Michael's Grammar School. Over a dozen students have attended your alma mater, St. Francis Prep High School, in your honor. You probably were laughing when they hung your basketball shirt in the gym there.

Michael, you did succeed. Your boys are beautiful, and Denise is doing a great job. You would be so proud of her and them. I know you are not the mushy type, but kiss and hug Maureen and Aunt Dee for me. Nana, Grandpa, Grandma, Pop, Betty and the rest of the family. Your spirit is alive because of our love for you and your love for us. I'll be with you in the future.

All my love,
Bernadette

Bruce D. Boehm

🍂

Bruce Douglas Boehm was born on March 8, 1952, in Rockville Centre, New York, to Charles and Dorothy Boehm, and had an older brother, Jeffrey. He married Irene Bilancia on September 11, 1982. Bruce earned a BA from Binghamton University and worked for Cantor Fitzgerald on the Government Agency desk. His greatest pleasures were his two children, Brittany and Stacey, and his wife, the beach, running and enjoying some beers on his deck at home with friends. On September 11, Bruce (aka Chappy) was at his desk on the 104th floor of the North Tower. He was forty-nine years old.

LETTER WRITER: Irene Boehm (wife)
AGE: 46

Dear Chap,
On the evening of September 10, 2001:

Your mom was frail and eighty years old.
Brittany had passed her driver's test and was very happy!!
Stacey was in seventh grade and was doing her homework . . .
Both the girls had swim practice, which ended early . . .
According to you, we were "living a charmed life!"
I was happily married to a man that I didn't realize how much
I loved . . .

53

On our nineteenth wedding anniversary, September 11, 2001:

Your mom was frail and eighty years old . . .
Brittany was sixteen . . .
Stacey was thirteen . . .
I was heartbroken . . .

In January 2011:

Your mom is frail but now she is ninety!! We just had a dinner
for her birthday.

Brittany is twenty-five and is a nurse at the Hospital for Special
Surgery in Manhattan. She lives in Manhattan. She has been an
ocean lifeguard (just like you!) at Jones Beach since she was seven-

teen. She has a steady boyfriend who is very nice. She has grown into a beautiful, independent, smart woman.

Stacey is twenty-two and is a nurse at North Shore Hospital in Manhasset. She is currently living at home. She has also been an ocean lifeguard since she was seventeen. She has run half marathons and even the marathon (just like you!) in Boston. She has also grown into a beautiful, independent, smart woman.

Both of the girls live each day to the fullest (just like you!). To say you would be undoubtedly proud of them is an understatement. You may not have been with them for a long time, but your imprint is certainly there!

I now work full-time (stop laughing!!). I have met many new people, and that is healthy for me. I am also a docent at the World Trade Tribute Center. I give tours of Ground Zero twice a month. I don't ever want the world to forget that awful day. The tours are painful, but therapeutic.

My best friends these days are four women who I never knew before September 11, 2001. Their husbands also worked for Cantor. We joke that "we wish we never had to meet." Yet they are the friends who comfort me the most.

For the most part, though, life for me is about going through the motions. There is a huge hole in my heart that will never heal. It just doesn't bleed as much anymore.

What has changed is that I now *realize* how much I loved you and still do . . .

Love,
Me

ANTHONY LUPARELLO

米

Anthony "Tony" Luparello was born on November 24, 1938, in Italy, to Santino and Provedenza Luparello, and was one of five children. Anthony came to America when he was eighteen and worked as a baker for thirty years, before starting his career with Allied Building Maintenance at the World Trade Center. Anthony was married to Geraldine for forty years and had four children, Maria, Geraldine, Anthony Jr. and Steven, who passed away in 1995. A loving husband, father and grandfather of six at the time, Anthony loved to go crabbing, play bocce, watch baseball, help his children with home-improvement projects and everything involving his grandchildren. At the time of the attack he was at work on the 101st floor of the South Tower. He was sixty-two years old.

LETTER WRITERS: Maria Theresa Lipari and Gina Lipari
(granddaughters)
AGES: 18 and 13

Dear Grandpa Tony,
You were sixty-two years old when you died, and had just celebrated forty years of being happily married to Nana. You had a wonderful life together, raising four children in Corona, New York, watching your children grow up and welcoming six grandchildren in your lifetime.

You and Nana did everything together: working around the house, shopping, cleaning, cooking, gardening. You just loved to be in each other's company. Every summer, you and Nana would come out to Long Island and take us to our secret spot to go crabbing. You would teach us how to pull in the lines the right way, and how to scoop up the crabs with the net. We caught dozens of crabs in just one day. When you got tired, you would sit on the buckets and pretend the crabs were pinching you. You always knew how to make everyone laugh.

We miss you, Grandpa. We love you.

Maria Theresa and
Gina

Anthony, Geraldine, Gina and Maria Theresa

SALVATORE P. LOPES

Salvatore P. Lopes was born on July 30, 1961, in Astoria, Queens, to Carmelo and Mary Lopes, and was the brother of Antoinette and Lenny. He married Lorraine Whelan in 1985 and had two daughters, Alexandra and Nicole. Sal attended Queensboro Community College before entering the Police Academy. He served as an NYPD officer for seven years prior to becoming injured. At that time he took courses and became a travel agent. Sal was passionate about baseball and loved the Yankees. His shining moment was watching them win the World Series in 2000. He delighted in coaching both his daughters' softball and basketball teams. He loved playing golf and being with friends and family. He particularly enjoyed his job at Sandler O'Neill & Partners, where he was the in-house travel agent on the 104th floor of the South Tower. He was forty years old.

LETTER WRITER: Alexandra Lopes (daughter)
AGE: 21

Dear Daddy,

Even though it has been ten years without you, your presence is still with me every day. You may have only been in the first eleven years of my life, but you really made them count. What seems the most shocking to the family is just how much I continue to have your personality. Sometimes Mommy and Mam just look at each other a little freaked out by some of the things I say and insist that it's something you have said or would have said.

Now that I have gone on to college, I have made many new close friends who will never know you. Usually, when I try to describe you to them, I tell the story of the last baseball game we attended together, on September 9, 2001.

Salvatore, Nicole and Alexandra

First, we stopped in Astoria, where you showed me the house you grew up in. It was the first time you had taken me there and showed me the places that were so important in developing the great man that you became.

The Yankees were playing the Red Sox that day. When we took our seats, you managed to stir up a conversation with a particularly brave woman who was wearing a shirt that read "The Yankees Suck" in the House That Ruth Built. I remember so clearly how you went up to her, not with anger, which many die-hard Yankees fans such as you would have done. Instead, you said, "Ma'am, I've gotta tell you, you have got *some* nerve to be wearing a shirt like that in this place! I actually admire you!" The two of you managed to crack rivalry jokes for the entire game.

Prepared for the chance of catching a foul ball, I had brought my mitt and I waited patiently for my chance. A few innings in, a ball was hit in our section. Being eleven, I was stunned when I saw dozens of men rummaging to get their hands on the ball. Somehow, the ball had bounced down into our section, into the hands of Uncle Marc, who came with us to the game. Uncle Marc happily gave the ball to me; even though you tried to make me give it back to him, he refused.

Suddenly our joy was disturbed when we discovered that the ball had bounced off the nose of another spectator. The man was quickly rushed to first aid for help with what appeared to be his broken nose. You explained to me how important it was to return the ball. Ultimately, it was the right thing to do. Although we were both disappointed, we returned the ball to the injured man, who was grateful for our kindness.

That day is just one example of how you taught me to become the person I am today, even though you have been absent for nearly half of my life. I guess that just goes to show what kind of impact you managed to make in the lives of the people you surrounded.

Your impact on my life has not and will not change. Even years from now, when I have a family of my own, and new people in my life who still did not get to know the great man who helped to mold me into the woman I have become, I will be sure to let them know you had a major role in my life. And if I am lucky enough, I can have the impact on them like you had on me, shaping them into driven, educated and loving people.

Love and miss
you always,
Al (your Pal)

RONALD T. KERWIN

Ronald T. Kerwin was born on October 6, 1958, in Hicksville, New York, to William and Carol Kerwin, and had two brothers, Kenny and Danny. He married Dianne Pressler in 1985 and had three children, Ryan, Keith and Colleen. Ronny started his career with the New York City Fire Department in 1981 and was a Lieutenant in Squad 288, Maspeth, Queens. Ronny also joined the volunteer fire service in 1982 and was Chief of Department of the Levittown Fire Department in 2000 and 2001. He adored his family and enjoyed fishing and golf. On September 11, Ronny and his company were evacuating the South Tower. He was forty-two years old.

LETTER WRITER: Glenn Pressler (brother-in-law)
AGE: 45

Dear Ron,

When I think back, there are a few dates that stand out in my mind.

The first date is Fourth of July week of 2001. We were standing outside Miller's cottages, and you were telling me you were going to work another year before retiring.

The next date is a couple months later, Labor Day weekend at my house. We took a picture of you and Dianne with the kids

Glenn (left) and Ronald

sitting on the steps in the porch. It's the last family picture we have of you.

The last date is a few months later, on December 7. I was at a holiday party when I received a call from Captain Brennan telling me they recovered your body. I left and drove to your house to tell Dianne. It was the hardest thing I have ever had to do.

Since your death, many things have changed. We all tried to help Dianne, especially with the kids, sometimes just answering questions or telling stories about you. But the family was changed forever. I saw not only how your death broke my sister's heart, but how it tore my parents' hearts out, feeling helpless as they tried to comfort their child.

I wanted to let you know that some of my favorite memories of my life include the great camping trips we had at Chamberlain Lake. I have some great pictures.

Your grave is not far from my office, and whenever I take the train into the city I stop by. Your death has made me think more about an afterlife. In the past, something I spent more time questioning than believing. I hope that some day we'll have time to catch up, when we meet again.

Love,
Glenn

MICHAEL BRADLEY FINNEGAN

🌿

Michael Bradley Finnegan was born on March 14, 1964, in Syracuse, New York, to Frank and Beverly Finnegan, and was the brother of Katherine. Mike married Erin in 1992 and had three children, Bridget, Bradley and Jack. He earned a BA in Economics from the University of Richmond. Mike's passions were his family, friends and golf. On September 11, Mike was working for Cantor Fitzgerald on the 104th floor of the North Tower. He was thirty-seven years old.

LETTER WRITER: Erin Finnegan (wife)
AGE: 46

Dear Mike,

We miss your hugs. We miss your kisses. We miss your laughter, your voice. We miss watching you putt golf balls in the living room. We miss admiring the way you talk to people. We miss reading with you before bed. We miss playing in the ocean with you. We miss your jokes and, most of all, we miss you. We miss all of you.

We know you are with us every minute of every day because we *feel* you. We sense your presence on our toughest days and our best days, and all the days in between. We *see* you when we look at each

Mike, Jack, Erin, Bradley and Bridget

other, at your parents, your sister and your friends; you live on in all of us. For that we are grateful. It seems like a lifetime since we've heard your voice.

Thinking of you . . .

Your hands. Your strong, graceful hands held our baby son Jack on each of your thirty-nine days together with enough tenderness to last a lifetime.

Your smile. When weren't you smiling? Your inner peace showed in that smile, in your eyes, simply warming those of us fortunate enough to be in your presence.

Your soul. You were a gift. People just liked you. We all gravitated toward you and wanted to be more like you. You didn't even know what you were doing because it came naturally to you.

Your memory. You live on, my love, in so many ways, in so many people. Our daughter, Bridget, has your uncanny ability to do things that I can't do. She just logically figures everything out. Like you, she rarely gets rattled, she knows who she is and she is so easy to be around, and yes, Mike, she is beautiful. You could say Bridget's wisdom is beyond her years, but I think it's in her blood. You were right, she's perfect. She also has your smile. Our son Bradley fortunately—and unfortunately—inherited your wild side. He is a thrill seeker, just like you were. As only God would balance it, along with the mischievous gene came the charming gene. Time and again, people young and old are drawn to him. He has your eyes. Our son Jack is magical. Whatever it was that made you so special just overflows in that little guy. Jack is loved by everyone, instantly. I could go on and on, but you know . . . Jack is happy. A good friend expressed to me one time that Jack didn't know loss early on; he only knew love . . . lots of love from so many, after you died. Love showed up on our doorstep every day, and still does to this day.

Your parents. We are so blessed to have them in our lives. When I watch the way they love and guide our children I know why you turned out so decent. They are so loving and patient, and accepting like you. They talk about you all the time.

I'll never forget the way we were. My heart will always feel you near me. I was so blessed to have you in my life even though it wasn't for long. The memories I have of our time together make me who I am today. You taught me so many things and I still keep our traditions. I tell our children stories about you and point out when they act like you. I try to do what you would do when I'm faced with adversity and even when I'm not. You taught me to visualize my golf shots; well, I visualize *your* golf swing before every shot I take. That helps my game. I continue to love life and try to live as freely as you did. I love you—and I miss you so much.

Until we meet again, kiddo, we will continue to smile like you. We love you to the moon and back and back again.

Erin, Bridget, Bradley
and Jack

KHANG NGUYEN

Khang Ngoc Nguyen was born on December 19, 1959, in Saigon, Vietnam, to Bich and Quy Nguyen, and was one of nine children. He and his entire family came to America in 1981. Khang married Tu HoNguyen on July 4, 1993, and had one son, An Ho-Ngoc Nguyen. Khang graduated with a BS in Electrical Engineering from the University of Maryland and was a few hours short of his master's degree from George Mason University. He worked for Science Applications International Corporation and was assigned to work as a Systems Administrator at the Navy Command Center in the Pentagon. He loved his family, playing soccer and tennis, and had a passion for playing guitar. On September 11, Khang was in his office on the 2nd floor of D Ring in the Pentagon. He was forty-one years old.

LETTER WRITER: An Ho-Ngoc Nguyen (son)
AGE: 14

Dear Dad,

I had just turned four years old when you were gone, killed in the terrorist attack while working in the Pentagon on September 11, 2001. My memory of you is vague. Our family photos and the stories from Mom help to keep your memory alive. I love you very much, even though you are not a part of my everyday life.

You loved working for the U.S. government at the Navy Command Center as a Systems Administrator, and I remember you devoured books on the military, particularly those involving the Vietnam War.

Early on that Tuesday morning, September 11, while Mom was seeing me off at the school bus in front of the house, you suddenly ran out and waved to me. You called out loudly, "An, say goodbye to Daddy one more time," while the bus was driving away, a gesture you had never made before. It was the last time father and son would see each other.

Some of our family members tell me that I am very much like you. I have the same body build and expressions, especially my smile. Like you, I am also good in math and science.

My favorite photo of us is the one taken on my third birthday. You let me sit on your shoulders and we laughed and looked so happy. In another one, we were at the park where you showed me

how to play soccer. It was a summer day and you and I were kicking the ball back and forth. I also like the picture of me wearing a military uniform that you bought for me from one of the stores inside the Pentagon.

Mom says that everyone in our family, as well as your friends and coworkers, love and miss you so much. You were smart, very kind, generous and willing to help people. You were also talented. Playing guitar was your greatest passion. Growing up in Vietnam, one of the poorest countries in the world, you had to sacrifice all of your meal allowances to buy your first guitar. You played it beautifully since your teen years. The most vivid memory I have is when I would go upstairs to bed and I could hear you in the living room playing very soft guitar music. I would go to sleep so peacefully. You told Mom that you would teach me to play the guitar when I turned five.

Now, I am fourteen years old. Sadly, you could not be here for my music lessons. I am saddened and sometimes angry that I was forced to grow up without a father. I have learned about terrorism and the war on terror. Mom told me that you hoped that I would volunteer to serve in the military when I grew up. To honor you, I will try my best to carry out your dream to protect our family and country.

You are my hero. You are always in my heart. I am so proud to be your son. I promise to be a good student and study hard so that when I become a man, I will make you, up in heaven, happy and proud of me.

Love,
Your son, An

BRENDA E. CONWAY

～

Brenda E. Conway was the first of twins born on February 19, 1962, in New York, New York, to William and Edith Alexander. She married Russell Conway and had two children, Danielle and Mandell. Brenda loved to shop and was known for wearing bright colors and her signature colorful socks. Brenda worked as a Systems Analyst for Marsh & McLennan on the 97th floor of the North Tower. She was forty years old.

LETTER WRITER: Linda McGee (twin sister)
AGE: 50

Dear Brenda,

It's hard to believe that you are gone. I miss you so much. What I miss most is our twin-ship. I miss one of us not getting our class picture because the photographer thought he took the same picture twice. I miss picking you up only to realize we were dressed the same and insisting that you change. I miss the stares and people always asking if we were twins. I miss our birthdays together and our endless telephone conversations. I miss you.

Nothing and no one can ever replace what we had. Being a twin was my life, and at times, I struggle to define myself without you. But we taught each other so much during our twin-life. It's the very words that you've spoken to me that keep me going. You have

Brenda (left) and Linda

taught me the power of education, so I completed college and went on to get my master's degree. You have taught me the uselessness of giving up, so I continue on despite opposition. You have taught me the power of prayer, so I pray continually for the strength of God to endure. I wrote a book about you and your struggle to learn how to read. It's entitled *B Is for Brenda*. It's the story you often told of how you were unable to read your name when you were in kindergarten.

Although it has been difficult to go on without my twin sister, there have been good days. I can laugh again, I can smile again. My life has changed so much, I am slowly moving on. You would be so proud of me.

You have three beautiful granddaughters now. I teach and instruct them just the way you would have. The kids are all grown up. It's hard to believe they are the same four little children that were packed into the backseat of my car every weekend. They are working, going to school and driving their own cars. We sure did a great job raising them.

Though you are no longer present, you live on through those of us who remain. Your love and memories remain in our hearts forever.

Your twin,
Linda

TOMMY LANGONE

✿

Thomas Michael Langone was born on July 19, 1962, in Roslyn Heights, New York, to Paul and Sheila Langone, and was the younger brother of Peter and older brother of Rosemarie and Joanne. In 1987, he married Jo-Ann Accardi, and they had two children, Caitlin and Brian. Tommy was employed by the New York City Police Department in their elite Emergency Services Unit, and he was a fire safety instructor for the Fire Service Academy in Bethpage. He was an avid volunteer firefighter and dog lover, and had a passion for teaching and spending time with his family. He was responding somewhere on or around the 20th floor of the South Tower on September 11. He was thirty-nine years old.

LETTER WRITER: Caitlin Langone (daughter)
AGE: 22

Dear Dad,

I remember your calm, steady voice saying, "Firecom 5602." I am in the back of a Chevy Tahoe that has been converted into an emergency vehicle, with my brother, Brian, seated beside me. We had known from the telltale shrill of a beeper that we were headed off to what was simply referred to as a "call."

I can recall sitting in the backseat, the giddy rise in my heartbeat, the racing of blood throughout my body, the overwhelming sense of excitement I later came to know as an adrenaline rush. Throughout the entire ride, your voice over the radio never wavered or quivered. It was steady, resolute and concrete. There was a job to be done.

Upon our arrival to the scene, you would leap from your seat with only one command for my brother and me: "Stay here." We obeyed; we understood that the situation that you were about to enter was not for us. Moving to the back of the truck, you pulled from a compartment all sorts of equipment. Patiently, Brian and I would wait until the squeal of sirens would break the silence. With the arrival of the ambulance, we knew it would be only moments until you returned to us. A sense of comfort would always wash over us once you were back in the car, casually jotting down information on the call sheet. When we were with you, everything was right with the world.

This was the norm for my childhood. Because you were the Chief of the Roslyn Rescue Fire Department, we were often whisked away on adventures. An average dinner was spent being regaled with stories of emergencies we had missed while you worked as an ESU cop in Queens. Back then, we spent all of our time at the firehouse. Back then, you were as strong as a mountain, taller than most trees, invincible like Superman and so much smarter, too. Your presence was the rock-solid foundation our family was built on. The greatest assurance to our young minds was knowing that you were there. While we were with you, we had no reason to fear anything. There was a feeling of absolute safety. It is because of this peculiar childhood that I listen to sirens with fondness. The shrill scream doesn't give me chills, nor does it indicate disaster in my mind. Instead, I smile to myself. The sirens make me think of you.

I wasn't there when you went on your last call. En route to your ESU truck, the call came over. With lights and sirens blazing, you sped toward the scene. I can't imagine what was going through your mind when you arrived and saw what had transpired. Unfalteringly, you ran into the chaos of 9/11. You and your partner saved hundreds of people from death that day, but you could not avoid your own. Neither could your brother, a city firefighter who had also responded. Disregarding the towering inferno, the work of terror looming before you, you ran back again and again with the tireless devotion, relentlessness and strength that drove you in life.

Brian and I are so lucky to call you our father. I miss you terribly, but I am so very proud.

Love,
Caitlin

CRAIG MONTANO

🌿

Craig Douglas Montano was born on October 27, 1962, in Queens, New York, to Richard and Catherine Montano, and was the brother of Ricky and Kevin. He married Caren Mercer in 1992 and had three children, Christa, Lukas and Liam. He earned a BS from Syracuse University and worked for Cantor Fitzgerald. He loved his family, friends and spending time at the beach or camping with loved ones. On September 11, Craig was at his desk on the 104th floor of the North Tower. He was thirty-eight years old.

LETTER WRITER: Caren Mercer (wife)
AGE: 49

Dear Craig,

I am writing this letter to you as a thank-you for all of the wonderful times we have shared together. We met as freshmen at Syracuse University in 1980, and we honestly just never stopped. Your friends became my friends, and mine yours. We were inseparable early on and had the most fun just being with each other and hanging out.

As I reflect back on our life together I am struck by all that you had accomplished and all that we have achieved despite your absence. Christa has your earnestness, intelligence and beauty. Like you, she loves adventure and trying new things. Lukas is the life of

Christa, Liam, Craig and Lukas

the party, just like his father, and is athletic and a loyal friend. He ends each telephone conversation with me by saying, "I love you"— just like you did. Liam is independent and gentle. He loves to snuggle and laugh and have fun. He has your silly sense of humor and is a great brother and son.

Somehow, in the short time we had together as a family, you were able to instill in our children some of your best qualities. Daily, I am struck by your presence.

Thank you for an amazing life with you. Thank you for our three amazing children, without whom I do not know how I would have had the strength to get through these many years without you.

After your death, I made a choice for our family. It was a choice I knew you would have made yourself. The choice was to go on and make it a good life. Despite our overwhelming sadness and grief over your death, our family is a good, strong one. We have the love and support of each other and of your family and mine.

Love Never Stops.
Caren

Paul F. Beatini

⚘

Paul F. Beatini was born on June 26, 1961, in Englewood, New Jersey, to Michael and Doris Beatini, and was the youngest brother of Michael, Thomas, Nanda and Mark. He married Susan Fischer in 1991 and had two children, Julia and Daria. Paul earned a BS in Chemical Engineering from the New Jersey Institute of Technology and worked for FM Global. He gave completely of himself to be with his family as much as possible. He loved cooking, eating and entertaining. On September 11, Paul was at a meeting at Aon in the South Tower. He was forty years old.

LETTER WRITER: Julia Beatini (daughter)
AGE: 14

Dear Dad,

One of my clearest childhood memories is working with you in the room we called "the Play-Doh Room," as it was the center of all our arts and crafts. There, we sat for hours shaping a block of clay into a bowl of fruit. I can still remember watching in awe as your big, strong hands carved every last intricate detail, down to the seeds on the strawberries. I can still remember your face, the passion in your eyes as you worked. I can remember being inspired, realizing at the age of four that, like you, I was meant to be an artist.

Never in a million years would I have guessed that just months later, on September 11, 2001, another day that I can remember as if it were yesterday, my entire world turned upside down.

The time after that was a blur of waiting and watching and crying. There were moments, especially on holidays, which were particularly horrible, moments when the air was thick with grief, when the lumps of sadness in the backs of our throats silenced the room. Often, to avoid this, someone would come up with a game to entertain everyone, especially me and Daria. My favorite was drawing contests; even in our worst moments, a drawing contest would always add some levity to family gatherings. For just a moment, drawing could take me back to the time before you died; drawing could take away some of the ache inside me. My art then was filled with bunnies and rainbows, flowers and sunshine: the direct opposite of how I felt.

Although I've since graduated from crayons to oil paints, I still find peace in art. Years later, I'm a long way from September 11 and even further away from the Play-Doh Room, but I still cherish the experience of creating something beautiful. Some days, I'm a typical teen who, because my beloved Johnny dumped me or my BFF betrayed me, uses drawing to heal. Other days when I spend two weeks crafting a watercolor of an iris or even, still today, a bunny, I have that passion that I first saw in your eyes. Even at my age, I've lived and learned life's greatest lesson that nothing is permanent, but I know I'll always have art.

I love you and miss you, Dad.

Julia

VALERIA MURRAY

Valeria Veronica Murray was born on September 15, 1935, in New York, New York, to Joseph and Helen Beres. She married Patrick Murray in 1955 and had five children, Valerie, Michael, Kenneth, Timothy and Veronica. Val was a Legal Secretary at Ohrenstein & Brown. She loved her family, playing board games and watching Clint Eastwood movies. On September 11, Val was traveling to work on the 85th floor of the North Tower. She was sixty-five years old.

LETTER WRITER: Tim Murray (son)
AGE: 46

Dear Ma,

"We believe in you. We love you. We honor you. We miss you."

Those words were spoken by Kenny at your memorial service almost ten years ago and still hold true today.

We love how you were able to shower us with your attention even while working a full-time job. We understand the tremendous sacrifices you made throughout our childhood, making sure that we did not go wanting even though we never had much money. And you always found the time to share special moments and talks with us.

We honor you in our thoughts and actions every day, and we take our children to church each Sunday to show respect to everyone in this world.

We miss your smiling face, great laugh and silly jokes. Miss you always being there for us whenever we needed you.

Although you were abruptly taken from us, we know that you are still with us in spirit and watching over our everyday lives. This past December, Mike had your 8mm home movies from the 1950s and 1960s put onto a DVD. For seventy-seven minutes, the DVD brought back many happy memories. Caitlin and Kylie had a great time watching you host parties as a newlywed, take the family to Coney Island and visit Babka's farm during our summer vacations. All of the fun trips that Ronnie and I took with you and Daddy in the 1970s came back in one tremendously happy dream. These trips and your everlasting love made us feel like a million dollars. Our childhood was truly remarkable, and it was all because of you.

Inevitably, our conversations during recent excursions turn to our special remembrances of you. Sharing laughs about getting lost around the Iwo Jima Memorial to your best Dick Van Dyke stumble/dance across a hotel room. We always, though, come back to that unforgettable visit to a Cape Cod lighthouse.

My girls love to hear stories about their Grandma Val. Monica and I wish you had more time on this earth with Caitlin and had had the chance to meet Kylie. To this day, I can see your sweet sensitivity in Caitlin and hear your unique laugh in Kylie. I can imagine you beaming with pride while watching Caitlin during her dance recitals or her showing you her latest artwork. I can dream of Kylie sitting next to you on the floor working on a jigsaw puzzle or playing a board game.

I'm not sure if we fully realized how much we learned from you until you were gone. We hope that you are proud of us as we continue to lead our lives in the way you taught us. We know that one day we will again get to share laughs together with you, Daddy and Kenny. Until then, please stay with us in spirit and continue to watch over us.

Ma, we believe in you. We love you. We honor you. We miss you.

Your loving son,
Tim

PAUL T. ZOIS

✻

Prokopios "Paul" T. Zois was born on April 25, 1955, in Athens, Greece, to Theofanis and Elizabeth Zois, and had his two sisters, Alexandra and Georgia. He came to the United States in 1965 and settled in New York. That same year, his wife's family came to New York from Poland. Paul married Dorota on October 3, 1981, and had a daughter, Stefania, on May 3, 1984, and a son, Theo, on June 24, 1986. Paul and Dorota worked for TWA and enjoyed traveling with their children. Paul's passion was coaching his children's soccer and basketball teams. He enjoyed manicuring the lawn, and was working toward his MBA from St. John's University. As a corporate Travel Manager for American Express, he was in the offices of Marsh & McLennan on the 94th floor of the North Tower when the first plane struck, minutes after speaking to his wife on the phone. He was forty-six years old.

LETTER WRITER: Dorota E. Zois (wife)
AGE: 53

Dear Paul,
You went to work on Tuesday, September 11, 2001, one hour earlier than usual. Just one week earlier, you changed your schedule so that you could be home in time to coach Theo's soccer team. Who could

have known that it would cost you your life? In reality, it wasn't the change in your work schedule that killed you. You were murdered senselessly by evil beings. An unforgivable act that changed us forever.

Above all things, you were the best father. Our children, Stefania, now twenty-six, and Theo, twenty-four, completed our life. They still do not have the full comprehension of the love, dedication and commitment that their dad had for them, that I now continue alone. It is with time and life experience that brings the wealth of wisdom full circle. There was not much that you did without them being foremost in your heart. Life revolved around them; what made them happy, what they enjoyed, where they liked to go,

what they liked to do. You were happiest when you did things for them, with them and about them. I know you are so very proud of them.

How often have I picked up the phone? I need to ask you something, what do you think about this or that? Did Theo tell you the score? Did Stefa tell you she made the honor roll? Did you hear? Well, did you? It is very rare that you come to me in my dreams, but when you do, you are always looking for our children, not me. It makes me sad, but then how else would it be? Your priority in life was always our children. It is from the heavens that you continue to look for them, their guardian angel. Always be our guardian angel.

Love,
Dorota

JAMES WARING

James "Jimmy" Arthur Waring was born on August 2, 1952, in Bronx, New York, to Richard and Catherine Waring, and was the brother of Helen and Mary Jane. Jimmy married Maria Fusco in 1985 and had four daughters, Jessica, Stephanie, Maria and Jamie. Jimmy enjoyed sports, music, the beach and friends. He played in a band; signed his name "Jimi" like his idol, Jimi Hendrix; and treasured his white Fender Stratocaster guitar. A Bronx native who rooted for the Chicago White Sox and Green Bay Packers since early childhood, he was truly one of a kind. Jimmy graduated from St. John's University with a BS in Criminal Justice. On September 11, Jimmy was working as Head of Security at Cantor Fitzgerald on the 105th floor on the North Tower. He was forty-nine years old.

LETTER WRITER: Jessica Waring (daughter)
AGE: 24

Dear Daddy,

We can't believe that it's already been ten years since the last time we saw you. Memories spent with you will always be treasured, and believe us, we are tremendously grateful for the number of memories we have of you, given the short amount of years we had you in our lives. It is impossible for us to forget a man of such character and personality, who was such an enormous part of our everyday lives. Happy twenty-fifth wedding anniversary; every year Mom misses her "buddy" even more.

We repeatedly wonder what our life would be if you weren't there that dreadful Tuesday morning, and we'll spend our lives wishing we could turn back time. All of those great things about you live on through us, your daughters who you loved so much: Jessica has your face, Stephanie your sense of humor, Maria your calmness and easygoing attitude, and Jamie your large piercing green eyes. You did a wonderful job raising us with Mom, and we are positive that you are very proud of what we've accomplished so far.

Jamie will never forget the time she swallowed a penny, and you turned her upside down and shook her by her ankles. Little Maria remembers the time she went into the bathroom to get ready for school and you put the plastic guard over the razor and pretended to shave her face. Stephanie remembers that to help her fall asleep, you used to scratch her back and write out letters with your finger on her back and make her guess what you were writing. Jessica remembers your love for classic rock, and the many times you dropped her off at middle school while you blasted the Stones, sang loudly and opened the car windows to embarrass her a bit. At the time she didn't appreciate how funny you were, but now she can almost hear your voice singing while she listens to your favorite Rolling Stones and Tom Petty songs. We frequently recall your famous one-liner that you often used to cheer us up—"Who's better than you? . . . Nobody."

We remember that you always carried a handkerchief with you—the one you had covered your face with when the World

Trade Center was bombed on February 26, 1993, as you climbed down 105 flights of stairs in the North Tower. Despite your asthma, you managed to help two elderly women down to their safety.

The most important lesson you taught us is to live life to the fullest; you certainly did. You truly appreciated your family, friends and the small things life had to offer. Most importantly, you cared about the well-being of others. We are certain that you were doing the best you could to help others when your life was taken on that terrible day, thinking of yourself last as you had always done.

Still to this day, our hearts ache with sadness when we think about you and how your life was unfairly taken. You should've had the chance to be here with us and to experience all of our achievements and milestones over the past ten years. We miss you tremendously, but we want you to know that we are living our lives to the fullest, just like you did.

Stephanie, Jessica, Jimmy, Jamie and Maria

You'll be glad to know that your favorite song was played at your memorial service:

Well, I won't back down . . . And I'll keep this world from draggin' me down. Gonna stand my ground and I won't back down.
                                                                    —*Tom Petty*

Your legacy lives on through each of us, and you will forever hold that special place in each of our hearts. No one will ever understand how much we truly lost on September 11, 2001. You are missed greatly, and we'll continue to miss you, until we meet again. Rest easy, Daddy. We know you are in a wonderful place now, watching down on us.

> Love always,
> Your daughters,
> Jessica, Stephanie,
> Maria and Jamie

MARK ZANGRILLI

~⟨

Mark Zangrilli was born on May 3, 1965, in Pequannock, New Jersey, to Emil and Rose Zangrilli, and was the brother of Linda, Richard, Karen and Kim. He married Jill Muccio in 1988 and had two children, Alexander and Nicholas. Mark earned his BA in Chemical Engineering from the New Jersey Institute of Technology. He loved to make people laugh, the New York Yankees and Long Beach Island. On September 11, Mark was in a meeting on the 105th floor of the South Tower. He was thirty-six years old.

LETTER WRITER: Jill Zangrilli (wife)
AGE: 46

Dear Mark,

Sometimes it only takes a sound or even a word someone may utter to suddenly bring us back to that moment, that hour, that day.

They say a man's most lasting legacy in this world is in the life he has lived, but I believe it is also in the lives he has left behind and the hearts he has touched. It is seen in the faces of his family and friends when they speak of him; it is seen in the love in their hearts when they think of him and in the courage it takes to go on without him.

We were told that time would heal, but time has never changed

Mark, Alexander, Jill and Nicholas

the way we feel. There is still heartache that lies behind the smile, and there are still days it is easy to break down and cry for a while, but then I think of you and your warm smile. I remember the kindness and generosity you gave without question, without limits. I remember your wisdom and strength. I remember a man who worked hard to accomplish his dreams. A man who embodied old-fashioned values like character and integrity. I remember the days you filled with jokes, laughter and fun. The times with your kids and the great love you had for each one. I remember the son, the brother, the father and the husband who was adored by his family.

We try not to hide behind the sadness and grief but somehow embrace it, by thinking of you every day with pride and love, knowing that the gifts you have given us have shaped our lives and the lives of our children. I see it every day when I look at them and who they have become. They are you, and I love that.

The legacy you left behind continues to grow. How truly extraordinary you were.

Forever,
Jill

JAMES NELSON

🍂

James Arthur Nelson was born on July 10, 1961, in Centereach, Long Island, to Bob and Catherine Nelson, and was the brother of Kitty and Bobby. James attended St. John's University on a fencing scholarship and graduated in 1983 with a bachelor's degree in Criminal Justice. In 1985, he began working for the Port Authority of New York and New Jersey Police Department. In 1989, James wed Rosanne Iuzzolino. By 2001, James had two daughters, Anne and Caitlin, and lived in New Jersey. James loved his family, his job, coaching his daughter's softball team and fencing. On September 11, 2001, James was at work at the Port Authority Police Academy in Jersey City when he was mobilized to the World Trade Center. James was one of the thirty-seven Port Authority police officers who did not make it out alive. He was forty years old.

LETTER WRITER: Caitlin Nelson (daughter)
AGE: 15

Dear Daddy,
So much has changed in the past decade: I'm not the little girl you remember—I've grown up a lot. Mommy says I'm just like you; I love the Beatles, I love to read, I love fencing. I'm not the only one who has gotten older. Anne is beautiful (I'll never admit it to her;

you know sisters) and she looks just like Mommy. Grandpa is ninety years old, if you can believe it, but he's nothing like he was ten years ago because of advanced Alzheimer's disease. Mommy is in her fifties (you didn't hear it from me).

My memories are fading and it hurts knowing they are slipping away, and I want to hold on to them forever. I'll never forget this one: September 10, 2001. We were in the living room, dancing with Mommy, then you played the song "Butterfly Kisses." You picked me up and danced with me. You said, "When you get married, I'm going to dance with you to this song at your wedding." Mommy told you it was getting late, and you carried me off to tuck me into bed. You kissed my forehead, and as you were walking to shut off the light, you turned around and said, "Goodnight, Caitlin baby, I love you. See you tomorrow."

I did see you the next day for the very last time. I woke up, I heard you getting ready for work, and I ran into the kitchen after you. I sat at the kitchen table with you while you ate breakfast. You put me back to bed and left for work, to be a hero and save the world.

You may not be here for every moment, but you are. You're in our hearts; you're watching over us. You're everything to me; you are bigger than a hero—you are a father who will never be forgotten. I hope you don't forget about me. I'm far away but I'll never let you go—I swear I'll be with you someday.

Butterfly Kisses
Always,
Caitlin

STEVEN F. SCHLAG

Steven F. Schlag was born on April 17, 1960, in Bronx, New York, to Donald and Patricia Schlag, and was the brother of Jean and Ellen. Steven married Tomoko and together they had Dakota, Garrett and Sierra. He graduated from Montclair State with a BA in Economics, allowing him to become a Senior Vice President in the securities section of Cantor Fitzgerald. He enjoyed skiing but also had a passion to help those in need, and there are many stories of that passion. Steve was on the 105th floor of the North Tower on September 11. He was forty-one years old.

LETTER WRITER: Don Schlag (father)
AGE: 74

Dear Steve,
How much I miss you. Now all I have are my memories of you.

The first time I saw you was when you were born and the doctor showed me to you. Although you could not see me, we stared at each other and I looked into your eyes, and it seemed you could also look into mine. The doctor remarked that he had never seen that before.

I love you and losing you will always be a stone in my heart.

Dad, forever.

Dan, Patricia and Steven

JAMES AUDIFFRED

🌿

James "Jimmy" Audiffred was born on November 29, 1962, in Elmhurst, New York, and had one sibling, Dolores, and several nephews and nieces (Adam, Melissa, Kaitlin, Mariah, Martin, Julia and Gladys). Jimmy married Robin and had one son, Jason. Jimmy worked for American Building Maintenance in the North Tower. His passion was lighthouses, and he loved to listen to music, spend time with family and travel to Maine to eat lobster. He was a very handy and creative man. He told silly jokes and made everyone laugh. On September 11, Jimmy was last seen on the 78th floor entering the elevator to escort patrons to Windows on the World in the North Tower. He was thirty-eight years old.

LETTER WRITER: Julia Senit Escobar (niece)
AGE: 12

Dear Uncle Jimmy,
When you died, I was two years old, so I really don't remember much. I remember you used to hold me in your arms and Spanish dance with me across the floor.

You were born in 1962 in Elmhurst Hospital. You spent most of your childhood living in Puerto Rico then returned to New York when you were in high school. You worked in the Twin Towers for eighteen years as an elevator monitor and cleaning the vents and waxing the floors.

You were a very successful man in daily life. You helped people through the good and the bad. You always offered help, love and care to many people in the world that you were probably not even close to. You

had a great smile, laugh, voice and personality. I wish I could see it on your face one more time just to let me know you care.

In my future, I expect to accomplish a lot. I plan on becoming a mortician, getting married and having kids. I plan on having nephews and nieces and always being there to catch them when they fall, like you did for me. I also plan to be there for my own children for any problems they would ever have, like a bad dream, failed test or a broken heart. No matter what it is, I will be there because I have perfect role models: you and Mom included.

You treated everyone with respect. I love you so much and always will, no matter what. I love you, Uncle Jimmy.

RIP Uncle Jimmy 1962–2001

I hope you will watch over us.

Love,
Julia

DONALD FREEMAN GREENE

~⁒~

Donald Freeman Greene was born on May 21, 1949, in White Plains, New York, to Charles and Phyllis Freeman, and had three brothers, Doug, Chuck and Steve. Charles died when Don was five, but he and his brothers were adopted by Leonard Greene when Phyllis Freeman remarried in 1958. Leonard's three children, Randy, Bonnie and Laurie, along with Leonard and Phyllis's child, Terry, increased the number of Don's siblings to seven. Don received his degree in Engineering from Brown University and an MBA from Pace University and worked at Safe Flight Instrument Corporation in White Plains, New York. He was an avid sailor, private pilot and skier; however, his greatest passion was for his wife, Claudette, and his children, Charlie and Jody. On September 11, Don was a passenger on United Flight 93. He was fifty-two years old.

LETTER WRITER: Bonnie Greene LeVar (sister)
AGE: 63

Dear Don,

You were an awesome brother. Remember when we first met? After your mom and my dad got married in 1958, we quickly became a family of seven active children (soon to be eight when Terry was

born). I remember you as an adorable nine-year-old eager to join in
whatever family fun was going on.

You were always playful, Donny,
but you also had a serious side. You
were naturally inquisitive and a
good student. I remember that your
bedroom wallpaper had a large map
of the world on it and you were
always "correcting" it. During the
1960s, countries in Africa went
through a lot of changes—and you
kept trying to keep up with those
changes—in ink! By the time you
left for college at Brown University, your wall was a complete mess!

You were a good friend, father, husband, brother and everything
else one could say about an exceptional person. And we all know
that you lived for your family. Charlie and Jody were an indisput-
able source of pride and joy to you.

Donny, it is ironic that you died on United Flight 93—in an
airplane, with our family's company's safety equipment on it. After
earning an engineering degree at Brown and an MBA at Pace University, you worked with Dad at Safe Flight Instrument Corporation, a leading manufacturer of aeronautical safety instrumentation
used in aircraft around the world.

Claudette, the love of your life, was such a wonderful wife and
is such a great mother. You thoroughly enjoyed your life and you
were always ready to show anyone who asked a recent picture of
Charlie and Jody along with sharing a new story about them.

The last time I saw you was on Thursday, September 6. We had lunch together and took our usual walk. You carried your dessert with you—a soft-serve yogurt cone—and, as you stopped to say something to me, a large monarch butterfly landed on top of the yogurt. We both stared—an unusual spot for a butterfly to land—and after what seemed a long time, it flew away. At the time, I thought it was a little eerie, almost like a messenger. You, being so pragmatic, bit off the bottom end of the cone and ate the yogurt from the bottom up.

You know the rest of the story.

If I were to speak for you, I think you would say:

Enjoy life. Be grateful for your family. And don't take anything for granted.

Love,
Bonnie

HARRY RAINES

🍂

Harry Arthur Raines Jr. was born on September 15, 1963, in Brooklyn, New York, to Harry and Gloria Raines, and was the brother of Joann, Joe, Ida, Gloria and Mark. As he predicted in his teens, Harry married Lauren Raehmann in 1990, and together they raised and loved three children, Jillian, Kyle and Kimberly. Family was everything to Harry, followed by the beach, football and his morning workouts. Harry was the Assistant Vice President of Global Networking for Cantor Fitzgerald. On September 11, he was in the North Tower. He was thirty-seven years old.

LETTER WRITER: Kimberly Raines (daughter)
AGE: 11

Hi Daddy,
I have seen pictures of us together and can see that you and I have an unbreakable bond. There were pictures where I was sleeping in your lap, me sitting next to you and ones where we were goofing around and having fun. These are simple things that my friends do with their dads but I will never get to do them

again. Don't feel like you abandoned us; I know you are here with me every day.

The two years I spent with you were wonderful. You were the best father in the whole world. I think of you every day. Thank you for being my guardian angel and protecting me from danger. It means a lot to me. Say hello to everyone, especially Joann; tell her that seeing her smile brightened my day. I can't even express how much I love you!

Love,
Kimberly C. Raines

Walwyn Stuart

꜡

Walwyn Wellington Stuart Jr. was born on February 13, 1973, in Brooklyn, New York, to Walwyn Sr. and Doris Stuart, and he was the youngest of seven children, Adolph, Diedra, Edwyn, Olga, Keisha and Monette. He married Thelma Lewis in 1997 and had a daughter, Amanda, who was born on September 28, 2000. He was passionate about his wife and daughter; he loved playing chess, performing magic tricks, sports and serving in several ministries at the Brooklyn Tabernacle Church; and he was loyal to family, friends and colleagues alike. His Christian faith was vital to his life. Walwyn studied for two years at SUNY Stony Brook prior to joining the New York Police Department in 1993. He had served in the Path Division of the Port Authority Police Department since 2000. He was possibly in the South Tower on September 11. He was twenty-eight years old.

LETTER WRITER: Thelma Stuart (wife)
AGE: 42

Dear Sweetheart,

Oh, how I miss you so very, very much. Walwyn, I miss your smile, your warmth, your hugs and kisses and even your attempt at singing. If only I could hear you clear your throat in preparing to sing (smile).

I miss seeing you interact with Amanda. She is growing up

quickly and beautifully. Her smile is as electrifying as yours was. Sometimes I get upset when I look at her, as she reminds me so much of you and how heartbreaking it is for me that you're not around to see her. I know how much you wanted to see her walk. Guess what? She walked four weeks after you died. She walks just like you. I'm often tickled when I see her walk with such boldness and speed as you did.

I am still videotaping her as you did, although at times I have slacked off. Thank you for making so many recordings of her. Every chance that I get, I share more of you with her, as she allows. I have tried very hard to remain strong for her. Amanda is extremely affectionate and loves to give hugs and kisses—just like her father. You've left a great legacy for her.

You would have been pleased to hear of all the heartfelt thoughts from your friends, family and colleagues. I've tried to encourage people to tell others how they feel, as tomorrow is promised to no one. You did that for me. You were not short on sharing how much you loved both Amanda and me.

Thank you for the life that we had together. Although short-lived, it was still amazing. I am still . . . forever yours.

Loving and missing you always.

Your Sweetie,
Annie
(Thelma Stuart)

DAVID S. LEE

🪶

David S. Lee was born on August 11, 1964, in Brooklyn, New York, to Watson and Siu-Lan Lee, and was the brother of Eddie and Richard. He married Angela in 2000 and was expecting his first child in 2002. David earned a BA from the University of Pennsylvania's Wharton School of Business and an MBA from Northwestern's Kellogg School of Management. He was a devoted Yankees fan, loved to play golf and looked forward to fatherhood. David worked at Fiduciary Trust International and on September 11, he was on the 94th floor of the South Tower. He was thirty-seven years old.

LETTER WRITER: Angela Lee (wife)
AGE: 45

Dear David,

Remember you were convinced that I was carrying a girl and wanted to name her Samantha?

"But what if it's a boy?" I asked. "What name do you like for a boy?"

After some deep thought, you came up with a name.

Well, I want you to know we had a boy, born several months after your death. His name is Ryan—the name you picked that day. I wish you were here to welcome him home with me.

Remember we wanted our kids to know how to swim because neither one of us learned as youngsters? Well, Ryan is committed to his weekly swimming lesson, and he *will* swim. I wish you were here to see him learn.

Remember the golf clubs you gave me for my birthday? Well, I am sure you are happy to know that I chose to learn to play. I wish you were here so we could play your favorite sport together.

I cook when time permits. Ryan always wants to get in on the action with me in the kitchen. No doubt he makes a mess, but it's a good training for him to gain cooking skills, as you had. I wish you were here as my food critic when I experiment with new recipes.

Remember you wondered when your brother, Eddie, will get married? Well, not only is he married, he has a daughter. Richard has a girl and a boy. Your mother misses your regular visits and the family gatherings that you often planned with her.

Needless to say, life without you isn't the same. Miss you very much.

With all my love,
Angela

Kris Romeo Bishundat

~€

Kris Romeo Bishundat was born on September 14, 1977, in Guyana, to Bhola and Basmattie Bishundat, and was the brother of Danita and Devita. Romeo came to the United States when he was two and a half years old and grew up in Waldorf, Maryland. He enlisted in the U.S. Navy soon after high school, served six years on the USS *Shreveport*, reenlisted and was working at the Naval Computer and Telecommunications Station at the Pentagon on September 11. He was twenty-three years old.

LETTER WRITER: Basmattie Bishundat (mother)
AGE: 52

My Dearest and Beloved Son "Romeo,"
You are still living in every breath I take, in my veins and in my inner soul. I want you to know how kind people have been to us the past ten years. I suppose you are living through others for us. Most important, the strength that I have gained from the pain of losing you is immeasurable.

As for your sisters, Danita is our guardian angel and protector. Devita is all you—looks like you, act likes you and lives like you. Your father has become a new man, a new person, a new husband and a new father. Without his love, your passing would have been a thousand times more difficult for me. I wonder what you would have been today. To cheer me up when I am crying, Danita reminds me of how much you loved me and that always make me smile because I know you loved me as much as I love you and nothing else matters.

Love always
and forever,
Mom

ANTHONY PEREZ

Anthony Perez was born on March 31, 1968, in Jamaica, New York, to Anthony Sr. and Maria Perez, and was the eldest brother of Scott and Brian. He loved his wife, Mary, and children, Anthony James, Alexis and Olivia. Anthony earned a BA from SUNY Old Westbury and worked as a Technical Specialist for eSpeed under Cantor Fitzgerald. He was a die-hard fan of the New York Islanders and Mets, and was a jokester who collected comic books. Anthony was at work on the 103rd floor of the North Tower on September 11. He was thirty-three years old.

LETTER WRITER: Olivia Perez (daughter)
AGE: 20

Dear Dad,
You were the greatest man I could ever know. I'm sure any girl who loves her father as much as I do would say the same, but from the short time I got to spend with you, I know you were the greatest person alive.

It was fifth period of my first year of middle school, and my orchestra teacher had finally given in to the constant questioning from my peers about what had happened earlier that day. Once she had muttered the words that the World Trade Center had been attacked, I felt a sinking feeling in my stomach—you had just gotten a job there. Later that day, when I got home, Mom cried for the first and only time, telling me that you will no longer be with me. This is my only memory from sixth, seventh or eighth grade, and it is a memory that will remain with me for the rest of my life.

In the past ten years, I've done so much growing up and even more teaching. I graduated high school and got into the college of my dreams, but neither was possible without learning my very first lesson on September 11: *Life is too short—chase your dreams.* After the terrorist attacks, I was cut off from all media outlets to avoid hearing about the terrible acts, but I did get my hands on an article about a forensic anthropologist working at Ground Zero trying to identify the human remains that were uncovered. Something inside me lit up, and ever since, I've had a desire to become a forensic anthropologist. I want to try to give a name and face to victims to help families gain closure through finding their missing loved ones. I've been convinced that I can find my own closure. I just know it's what you would want me to do. Every hour I spent in the lab for forensic anthropology and human skeletal anatomy courses, I felt your presence. I always knew you were proud of me.

Dad, I miss just hanging out with you, Anthony James and little Alexis. Since you were always such a big Star Wars fanatic, you passed on your passion to us. Anthony James used to say to you, "Watch a Star Wuhz!" and you would run around yelling and tickling us. You always made a joke of the little things, and I absolutely adored the short amount of time we had together. It is funny, though: Trying to pick a single memory is like asking someone to pick her favorite dream. These memories are dreams that I hold close to my heart to keep me going.

I know that the children of Tuesday's Children will one day

grow up to become the leaders of the free world and make great changes in the world, but I just want to help families find their loved ones, to have something tangible to bury. Eventually, I can say that I've fulfilled my life and be very proud of myself. Out of the darkness comes light, and the kids of 9/11, my friends who I call family, will light the darkness and make the nation shine. But if I could ask for anything, it'd be one measly meal at a diner with you to talk about life, and what heaven's like, and how you and all my friends' parents are getting along.

Most of all, I'd like to hug you one last time.

I love and miss you dearly,
Olivia

DAVID G. CARLONE

✴

David Gary Carlone was born on December 17, 1954, in Waterbury, Connecticut, to Joseph and Anna Carlone, and was the brother of Joan, Nicholas, Joey and Paula. In 1977, David graduated from Bentley College earning a BS. On June 7, 1980, David married Beverly Deschino, and they had three sons, Darrick, Nicholas and Matthew. David was a devoted family man, a lifetime New York Yankees and Giants fan, a marathoner and a lover of ice cream. On September 11, David, an Account Executive for FM Global, arrived on the 105th floor of the South Tower at 8:30 a.m. to attend a meeting. He was forty-six years old.

LETTER WRITER: Beverly D. Carlone (wife)
AGE: 53

My Dearest David,

It was a weekend in November of 2002 when hope crossed my path for the first time. Thirteen-year-old Matthew, the youngest of our three sons, and I were coming home from a state cup soccer game. Just ahead, a group of deer slowly began to make their way across the road. Slowing our approach to a crawl, we began counting: one mother, two babies, a second and a third mother, three more babies, a fourth mom, and lastly . . . we looked at each other and exclaimed, "A goat!" Creeping closer, what we originally thought was a goat was in fact a young, pure white deer.

It wasn't until five days later at a support meeting that I realized I was blessed to have seen this white miracle. At this particular session, the "Legend of the White Buffalo" was read. I almost fell off my chair when I heard the words "white buffalo . . . symbol of purity . . . sent by the Great Spirit." Instantly, I found the correlation between the white buffalo legend and my own experience with the white deer, now named Hope.

On two occasions, I was able to take Hope's picture. The first time, daylight was quickly fading and the distance was far, but I was still able to capture Hope. Another time, there was a fresh blanket of snow, and just along the edge of the woods, there was Hope with her family. I was able to take several pictures before the group went deeper into the woods. Once developed, the photos revealed no presence of her.

I now realize how important it is to cling to hope even on days when life seems at its lowest. I believe my meeting this little white deer was not just a coincidence. This precious, white miracle is a symbol of hope for a purer, more harmonious world to come. On tough days, I seek out this gift from God along that country road. Although I do not always see Hope, like the picture in the snow, I whisper, "Hope, I know you are there, but sometimes you are just difficult to see."

Our oldest, Darrick, has followed your dedication to running and has completed his third marathon and will be running the Boston Marathon in 2012. Nicholas has graduated Army boot camp and completed his specialized training and is currently stationed in Germany. Matthew set a goal of achieving a perfect score for math on the SATs, which he accomplished! Matthew is thriving at Johns Hopkins University and will be graduating in 2012, majoring in Economics. For me, I call myself a "professional volunteer." I devote all of my time to the church and to many charities.

With a deeper sense of faith, I stopped dwelling on the "what-ifs" and the "what-onlys." A weight has been lifted from my shoulders and I now have a sense of inner peace. I approach life now with a positive attitude, one of faith and hope. It is easy to hold on to feelings of anger and hatred, but harboring such negative emotions only hurts one's self and those surrounding you. May we, as individuals, and as a nation, learn to "let go" such negative attitudes and may the warmth in our hearts grow to create a contagious circle of caring from sea to shining sea.

Ten years ago, an unthinkable act of hatred devastated our nation and our family. Although you were physically taken from me, David, I will always carry your spirit and your contagious enthusiasm for life in my heart, something that no one can ever take from me.

I never imagined living without your smile. Forever in my heart, patiently waiting until we meet again.

Loving you always,
Your wife, Beverly

WILLIAM FALLON

᛭

William Lawrence Fallon Jr. was born on September 20, 1962, on Long Island, New York, to William Sr. and Elizabeth Fallon, and was the brother of Elizabeth and Kenneth. He earned a BS in Computer Science from the Polytechnic Institute of New York in 1984 and an MS in Computer Science from the New York Institute of Technology in 1991. He married his high school sweetheart Laura Wesely on June 16, 1984, and lived in Coram, New York. Their daughter Kathleen was born on July 12, 1990, and Kayla was born on May 29, 1993. Bill's interests included running, cycling, travel and anything that involved fun with his daughters. He was Manager of Technical Support for Cantor Fitzgerald and was in his office on the 103rd floor of the North Tower on September 11. He was thirty-nine years old.

LETTER WRITER: Kayla Fallon (daughter)
AGE: 17

Dear Daddy,

I write this letter as my English class is discussing September 11, 2001. For many, it is just another sad story, but to me, it is where the road between my old life and my new one began. My old life involved seeing you every day: my father, my guardian, my best

friend. My new life is different. Instead of simply seeing you, now every day I live for you.

September 11 is slowly fading for some people. To me it is becoming more and more vivid as my knowledge of that day and the entire world grows deeper each and every day. Now instead of simply having a guardian I have a guardian angel. I know that you will never be forgotten in my heart, and I pray that it is the same for many others.

Thank you for changing my life. Continue to change it through your ever visible presence to me. I love you so very much and know that the day we meet again will be one of everlasting joy.

> Till forever,
> Your daughter,
> Kayla

RANDY SCOTT

🦢

Randy Scott was born on May 27, 1953, in Brooklyn, New York, to Lillian Scott, and was the brother of Bonnie-Ann, Jacqueline, Georgia and Deborah. He married Denise Castiglioni in 1979 and had three daughters, Rebecca, Jessica and Alexandra. He enjoyed golf, riding his motorcycle, the Yankees, coaching his daughters, and family vacations. Randy was an International Money Market Manager, Broker/Dealer beginning his career in 1975 at Lasser Brothers. On September 11, Randy was at his desk at Euro Brokers on the 84th floor of the North Tower. He was forty-eight years old.

LETTER WRITER: John McDonough (brother-in-law)
AGE: 74

Dear Randy,

I last spoke to you at 8:55 a.m. on September 11, 2001. You asked if I had heard that a plane had hit 1 WTC. I told you that I was searching on the radio for any news. Then there was an announcement over the PA system in your building that I could hear:

Please stay in the building. This building is secure.

I was in my office at 150 Broadway, just a short distance away. Remember I told you I was riding down to the street, to see what was happening. And you said you were working on a trade and staying at your desk. I remember you telling me that you intended to call the school in Stamford where Denise teaches, just to let her know that you were okay.

It was the last time we spoke. A second plane hit 2 WTC at the 83rd floor. You worked on the 84th. Approximately twenty-eight hundred individuals left this planet with you on that day of infamy. You were forty-eight years old and you left behind your wife and three daughters, ages eighteen, fifteen, and eleven.

We first met when you were just four, when I started dating your oldest sister, Bonnie, who would become my wife. Sadly, you and I shared the pain of losing her less than a year before I lost you. Bonnie and I could not have children, and I often said that you were the son I never had.

I like to believe that you are in a place where you are aware of

John (left) and Randy

the happenings here on earth, but just in case, I will fill you in. Your wife and daughters have been through enormous sadness and pain, but they are now better than they were, or so it appears to me. The four women are wonderful people, and you would be, or are, so very proud of them. Your daughters have established the Randy Scott Memorial Golf Outing at Sterling Farms in Stamford, with proceeds going to college-bound students in town.

Your daughters have not met "Mr. Right" yet, but honestly, you are a tough act to follow as a father. They are all beautiful. Obviously, inheriting their looks from their mother. Denise's parents moved to Stamford, and we are all pleased that they are close to your family. Your three living sisters and their children have all mourned your passing.

You had charisma and I never heard anyone say an ill word against you. May I say again that you are so missed by all who knew you.

Your loving
brother-in-law,
John

HASHMUKH PARMAR

🌿

Hashmukh C. Parmar was born on January 3, 1953, in Nairobi, Kenya, to Chakulal and Revakuvar Parmar, and was the brother of Dhiru and Manoj. He married Bharti in 1981 and had two children, Rishi and Shamir. Hashmukh earned a BS in Electronics Engineering from the University of Surrey, Guildford, England, and worked for Cantor Fitzgerald. He had a passion for music, playing instruments, and sports. He devoted most of his time to his family. He played an important role for his sons from coaching basketball and soccer to teaching them how to play guitar. On September 11, he was on the 103rd floor of the North Tower. He was forty-eight years old.

LETTER WRITER: Rishi Parmar (son)
AGE: 26

Dear Dad,

I lost you when I was just sixteen, and now I'm about to turn twenty-six in a few days. I will never forget the morning of that September 11. It started off just like any other morning, with you driving my brother and me to school. Never did it cross my mind that this was the last time I would see you. I remember slamming the door shut and then seeing the car speed off into traffic.

I was in English class when the principal came on the PA. He stated that there had been some sort of attack on the World Trade Center and that anyone with concern should report to the auditorium immediately. At first, I wasn't sure if you worked there, but then remembered you had recently taken a new job at one of the towers. I quickly left the classroom and found my brother on the way to the auditorium.

We tried calling you on your cell phone and office line several times, but nothing was going through at that moment. The next few days, family and friends were coming in and out of the house and we soon began to think the worst. A few weeks later, the worst came to reality when you never did make it back home.

You were there for me in every aspect of life. You helped me with homework every night, attended all my athletic events and shared the love of music with me. At first it was very hard, but I pushed myself to keep doing well in school and excel in athletics as I knew this is what you would want.

Music was something else you had taught me. For the past four years, I have been writing and recording a tribute song in memory of you. I have been releasing each song around the anniversary of September 11. This is my way of talking to you and letting you know how I am doing. At the same time, it also helps me get some of the pain off my chest. Others who have been through a similar experience can easily relate to these songs, and in turn, it may even help them, too.

Hope you've been able to hear the songs I made for you. I miss you and think about you every day.

Rishi

Scott McGovern

Scott Martin McGovern was born on November 29, 1965, in Brooklyn, New York, to Martin McGovern and Elisabeth Scott, and was the brother of Tara. He married Jill Shaffro in 1995 and had two children, Alana and Nicole. Scott earned a BS in Business from SUNY Albany, and had completed the first two of three levels on his way to becoming a Chartered Financial Analyst. Scott worked for Euro Brokers. He loved his children, his wife, his friends and his family with all his heart. Scott was an Oakland Raiders fan, played golf and enjoyed the company of many good friends. On September 11, Scott was at his desk on the 84th floor of _____ thirty-five years old.

LETTE_____ (wife)
AGE: 4

Dear Scott,

How is it possible that ten years have passed since I last saw you? That morning, that dreadful morning, is the day that our little girls lost the best dad in the world. Taking them outside to wish upon a star, doing puzzles, putting them in the wheelbarrow in the summertime and running around the block . . .

Why is it that when I think of you, it still brings tears but also brings such a smile to my face?

I have tried so hard to look beyond the sadness because I know that would be what you would want. Through conversations and letters I have received over the years, I have learned so many "new" stories about how you helped people, how much they treasured your friendship, how you truly made a difference in their lives. I can only hope that you knew that when you were here.

Your friends have done you well. The annual golf tournament that they hold each year in your memory is a testament to not only the person who you were, but to the people you chose as friends. They do this every year, to keep your memory alive. For many, many years to come there are children who will benefit from the scholarships that exist in your name at your alma mater, SUNY Albany. And because you were such a loving dad of two little girls, additional monies have been donated to a local hospital to purchase equipment for their pediatric wing. Also, funds have been used to help a children's hospice program. You see, Scott, you are not here in person, yet you keep on giving.

My heart breaks that you do not get to see the girls as they reach new milestones, but in my heart I know you are there. You have to be. And that mysterious empty seat near me at almost every recital . . . can you explain that? Maybe you can.

How blessed I am that you chose me to be your partner for the time you were here.

Scott, there is no way for me to be okay with what happened to you on September 11. It will never be okay. It has taken me a very long time but I have come to accept it. I look toward the future. I look at the two beautiful girls you left behind. What an amazing legacy; you would be proud beyond words as to their character, their intelligence, their strength and their accomplishments. They know so many "Daddy Stories" and will continue to have you in their life.

As you used to sign the cards you gave me . . . I say to you,

Love you madly,
Jill

John J. Tipping II

꽃

John J. Tipping II was born on January 4, 1968, on Long Island, New York, to John J. and Arlene Tipping, and had three sisters, Arlene, Maureen and Stephanie. John was a firefighter at Battalion 9, Engine 54, Ladder 4 in Manhattan. He enjoyed biking, the Hamptons and being with family and friends. John worked the night before the attacks. On September 11, his company was one of the first to arrive at the scene. All fifteen firefighters perished. He was thirty-three years old.

LETTER WRITER: Maureen Tipping-Lipshie (sister)
AGE: 38

Dear John,
About a month after September 11, I decided to write a journal. I had to find some way to express my feelings. Here is that first entry:

I have spoken to you so many times; I hope you have heard me. I have begged you to come home; the pain is so overwhelming it takes your breath away. I can't even imagine not seeing you again; sometimes I feel as if I can't move on or want to. I am not happy and wonder if I ever will be again. There is so much pain around

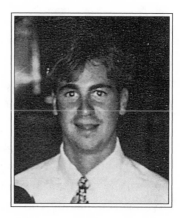

all of us. I can't let you go, John, I miss you so much. I don't think I am strong enough to handle this, I am sorry I am so weak. I am so sad.

Well, I have made it ten years. I remember wondering how I would make it through the day. I still cry easily when I think of you and of that horrific day. I will never accept the loss we have had to endure, but I have found ways to cope. Can you believe that Spenser is finishing college, Chase is in his first year, Sloane and Seaver are busy with school and soccer, Seth made assistant superintendent and I continue to save little kids as a school nurse?

In the months following 9/11, I moved from my house of ten years and started a new job. In September 2002, me, Dad and two of your brothers-in-law (one an NYC firefighter, the other an NYC police officer) rode our bikes from Ground Zero to Washington, DC, along with approximately two thousand other riders. It was quite an accomplishment and, to this day, brings back some very positive and emotional memories.

Dad still has his occasional bad days, but Mom is like a rock. I think her strength gives us all comfort. I don't know how she does it, but I am thankful for it. Your two nephews have a lot of you in them and that always makes me smile. I am grateful for anything that brings you a little closer to us.

I miss you so much, John. I continue to pray for strength, understanding and the health and safety of the family. I never used to think of the future, as it hurt too much, but I do know that I have many things to be thankful for and that the future holds many great things. I'm looking forward to all of those wonderful events. I love you and miss you, John, always.

Love your sister,
Maureen

MICHAEL V. SAN PHILLIP

🌿

Michael V. San Phillip was born on November 16, 1945, in Bronx, New York, to Salvatore and Rose San Phillip, and was the brother of Carolyn. Michael married Lynne Gorman in 1966 and had two daughters, Jill and Carrie, and four granddaughters, Mikki, Sarah, Lilly and Charlotte. Michael and Lynne celebrated their thirty-fifth wedding anniversary two months before Michael's death. He graduated from the University of Pennsylvania's Wharton School of Business in 1967. Michael's greatest love was his family and his passions were tennis, paddle tennis, golf and volunteering in his community. He was Vice President, Equity Sales and Trading, with Sandler O'Neill & Partners on the 104th floor of the South Tower. He was fifty-five years old.

LETTER WRITER: Mikki Abbott (granddaughter)
AGE: 9

Dear Poppa Mickey:
On September 11, I was still in Mommy's tummy. When I came out three months later, I was looking for you but I did not see you. From then on, I only could see photos of you. I see your picture every day on the table in our foyer with an American flag and a small steel cross from Ground Zero.

When I was in preschool, my teacher told the class what had happened on September 11. When I got home from school, I asked Mommy if that is what happened to you. Mommy was crying and I started to cry, but she told me that you were in heaven, and that you loved me before I even knew you.

Mommy told me how much you loved your girls and now you have four beautiful granddaughters. I am your first. My name is Michele, named after you, and I go by Mikki since your nickname was Mickey. I tell Mommy all the time that I met you, and I feel like you gave me a hug.

I wish you were here to teach me how to ride a two-wheeler, and how to play tennis like you taught Mommy.

I wish you were here right now.

I love you,
Mikki

MICHAEL GOGLIORMELLA

Michael Gogliormella was born on January 16, 1958, in Brooklyn, New York, to Mike and Connie Gogliormella. He married Daniela D'Arienzo in 1985 and had one daughter, Gillian. Michael earned a BS in Computer Science at Brooklyn College and worked for J.P. Morgan for eighteen years, and then for Cantor Fitzgerald. Michael loved his wife and adored his seven-month-old daughter. He was an avid skier, a passionate golfer and a huge fan of the New York Giants and Yankees. His life is a tribute to love, honor, integrity and courage. On September 11, Michael was on his way to his office on the 103rd floor of the North Tower. He was forty-three years old.

LETTER WRITER: Daniela Gogliormella (wife)
AGE: 49

Dear Mike,
The calendar tries to convince me that it wasn't just yesterday when you kissed us goodbye and hurried to catch the train.

Your final gift to me is now ten years old. She laughs like you—contagiously—and her big hazel eyes tell me everything—just like yours did.

I miss you. Remember how we used to read to each other at

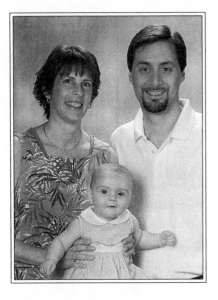

night? For a long time, all I did was cry at night, sobbing, smothered, choking, exhausted. I would stand in your closet and inhale, breathing, gasping, longing, fusing the scent to memory.

Remember how we watched movies every weekend until all hours of the night? I've forgotten now which movies you have seen, and which I've seen since you. Remember how you always kissed me in the middle of a car wash? Remember how you made us pancakes every Sunday morning and each week I'd tell you that they were the best pancakes you've ever made? I smile when I think of that.

Remember how we wrote our names in the cement of the sidewalk of our new home? They're still there. I found the rocks you painted white in the garage, with the words "M loves D" on them. That was a nice surprise.

At our wedding, I vowed "to love and honor you all the days of my life"; that was "my" life, not yours, and so I still do. Death took you, but love stayed.

I've worked hard to heal. Now I no longer sob myself to sleep, or wake with shocking impact. I make pancakes. I drive through the car wash with Gillian, reach back and tickle her knees.

I watch G-rated movies with computer-generated graphics, in 3D, and I'm asleep by 10 p.m. I attend parent-teacher conferences instead of riding the train to work. Disney trips have replaced Paris, but now we take our shoes off at the airport.

I saved some of your clothes, even the handkerchiefs. I can no longer smell you, except from memory. And to this day, your black Keds sneakers remain in the shoe cubby of our laundry room, like a dog waiting for its master's return. Despite the time that has passed, and the healing that has transpired, I just can't bear to move them.

I also know how much you loved me. You are my hero. Your influence on my life is profound and endures the passing of time. Thank you for teaching me about "more than anything, and no matter what." Thank you for "amazing."

Gillian has delivered. She is a full spectrum of adventure, and parenting is both the joy and challenge we expected. I wish I could have shared this rewarding part of life with you.

The pain has subsided. Time has healed me. But scratch the surface, and it's all still right there. The missing of you is daily, at large momentous occasions, and in incongruous or seemingly insignificant times of the day.

Now a different man—also a good man—is part of our family. He shares our joys, our dreams, our disappointments, and he cares for us. He buys me flowers, plays basketball with Gillian and tells us he loves us. His wife is somewhere in your world, waiting for us, like you. Comfort, understanding and peace have returned to me.

Joy—both welcomed and disguised—has snuck in.

And I still miss you.

Love,
Daniela

ROBERT CHIN

🕊

Robert Chin was born on June 30, 1968, in Brooklyn, New York, to Pak Ho and Yuet Ling Chin, and was the brother of Suk-Tan. He earned a BBA from Baruch College and worked for Xerox at the client site of Fiduciary Trust. Robert loved his family and friends, baseball, karaoke and photography. He was known as the "unofficial photographer" of Fiduciary Trust. On September 11, Robert was at work on the 97th floor of the South Tower. He was thirty-three years old.

LETTER WRITER: Suk-Tan Chin (sister)
AGE: 51

Dearest Robert,

I am looking at the awe-inspiring photograph that you took of the Peace Banner at the World Trade Center in 2000—the last holiday season there. Among the photographs of the peace sign that you took at the WTC every year, this was the most magnificent—a red banner hanging from up high, above the elevator doors in the lobby of the South Tower, with the word PEACE written in many, many languages.

Roberta Hope, my daughter and your niece and namesake, is six years old now. I was blessed to have been able to adopt her from China as a single mom. She is the new hope and she takes after

you. Like you, she loves playing ball and making friends at the park. She is fascinated by your softball trophies, your Yankees shirts that I now wear and the Mets opening day baseball that she found with your baseball cards.

"I wish I could see Uncle Robert," she cried, "and give him a kiss and hug. I cannot kiss a picture! I cannot hug a picture!"

Words of an innocent child, a child with your legacy. What amazement I felt when I adopted her, when I learned that she was born on 9/11, according to the Chinese calendar.

On September 11, you went to work and disappeared into thin air, last seen on the 97th floor of the South Tower. Frantically I searched for you in the city, but you had become the very air that we breathe. Although you are gone, your spirit of love, laughter and kindness will live on in the people you'd touched, and that you continue to touch. Shine on, my sweet brother! You will NEVER be forgotten.

Love always,
Your big sister,
Suk-Tan

Marcello Matricciano

🌿

Marcello Matricciano was born on July 1, 1970, in Astoria, New York, to Umberto and Mirella Matricciano. He married Rosie Morales on January 20, 1993, and had a son, Nicholas Anthony, on August 11, 1997. Marcello earned his BA in Finance from Baruch College and worked for Cantor Fitzgerald's eSpeed Division as a Product Manager. He was a loving husband and a hands-on father, often getting up for those midnight feedings and diaper changes despite having to work the next morning. He loved cycling and his riding trips from Astoria to Central Park. He enjoyed dining out at the best restaurants and spending quality time with his wife and son. On September 11, Marcello was in his office on the 103rd floor of the North Tower. He was thirty-one years old.

LETTER WRITER: Nicholas Matricciano (son)
AGE: 14

Dear Dad,

I wish you were here just so that I could tell you that I have never, and never will, forget about you because you were as great of a father as someone could ask for. You helped me through times when I was sad, cranky and scared. I look back at pictures of when I was only a baby and you held me in your arms. I still keep a portrait of you in my room to remind me of you. Through all of the good times and the bad, I still love you as the great father you were.

No matter how many years I live, I won't forget you. I don't remember too much from when I was four years old, but having you as a parent is something I simply can't forget. Nonna Mirella and Nonno Umberto still tell me about their memories of you and how much they miss you. Mom and the three of us still reflect on how much we love you.

I hope that you are looking down on me right now and feel the same way about me, even though it has been nearly ten years. You were always there for everyone in the family, and we miss you. We may mourn, but please know that you will never be forgotten by any of your loved ones.

Love your son,
Nicholas

(aka Freshie—I still
remember that this is the
name you used to call me)

GREGORY REDA

彬

Gregory Reda was born on December 19, 1967, in Brooklyn, New York, to Frank and Ursula Reda, and was the middle child between John Michael and Christopher. Gregory married Nicole S. Fernandez in April of 1995. They had two children, Nicholas Gregory, born on Valentine's Day of 1999, and Matthew Antonio, born in July 2001. Greg was a family-oriented man who loved science and watching movies, and had a great passion for peanut butter. Greg earned a BA in Management Information Systems and an MS in Computer Science from Pace University. He was a Vice President for Marsh & McLennan. On September 11, Greg sent several text messages after the planes struck the World Trade Center. He was on the 95th floor of the North Tower. He was thirty-three years old.

LETTER WRITER: Nicole S. Reda (wife)
AGE: 38

Dearest Greg,

It barely seems possible that so many years have passed, and yet at times it feels like a lifetime since I heard your voice or felt your touch.

Although you may not be here physically, there are reminders

Nicole, Gregory, Nicholas and Matthew

of you in my every day and on special days, too. I see you in the chestnut eyes of your little boys. Nicholas's passion for science and Matthew's sense of humor are yours. Nicholas's love for peanut butter and Matthew's wavy hair are sweet reminders of you, too. I have received your signs and know that you are close by. I found the dimes; I've heard your footsteps. I have seen your reflection and smelled your aftershave. I see our numbers and catch our songs. My beliefs are stronger and my spirituality is enhanced.

During the past ten years, I know that you and God have helped me through and, at times, even carried me along the way. I know you were at Matthew's baptism and the boys' First Holy Communions. I received your sign while in the ER for Nicholas's broken bones. For the many birthdays and the every days, I know you were there with us.

You are remembered and cherished. I thank you for continuing to be in my life. I thank you, with all of my heart, for blessing me with the greatest gifts, Nicholas Gregory, now eleven, and Matthew Antonio, now nine. They have grown so very much. They are kind, thoughtful and loving boys that I know you would be proud of.

Ten years have passed and the echoes of you fill me with peace. I love you more than words.

Always,
Nicole

ROBERT LOUIS SCANDOLE

Robert Louis Scandole was born on February 9, 1965, in Brooklyn, New York, to Robert and Margret Scandole, and was the brother of Christopher. He married Sheila O'Grady in 1997 and had two daughters, Emma and Katie. Robert earned a BA and an MBA from St. John's University, and worked for Cantor Fitzgerald. His greatest love was his family; he was a huge fan of the New York Knicks and Mets. He enjoyed his summers in Breezy Point, especially Sundays at the Sugar Bowl and hot days at the beach. On September 11, Rob was at his desk on the 104th floor of the North Tower. He was thirty-six years old.

LETTER WRITER: Emma Scandole (daughter)
AGE: 14

Dear Dad,

I was only four when you left us, but I can still remember that dreadful day when I found out my father was unfairly taken from me. Ever since then, I have been finding ways to cope and ways to keep you alive. Every night, I silently pray to you and hope that you are proud of who I am so far. I'm now thirteen, turning fourteen in a matter of days; my teenage years without you will be hard, because now is when I am starting to figure out just who I am and I need all the guidance I can get.

You always had high hopes for me, expectations that seem impossibly high. When I was only a week old, you went out and bought a book called *See Jane Win*. The book was supposed to be a guide to help raise a successful daughter; I can see why you bought it. After all, I was your first child. I have full confidence that you didn't need that book. In the little time I knew you, there is one thing I'm sure of: You were a great friend, son, uncle and husband, and a wonderful father.

Our family has gone through some bad times, but your loss was by far the worst. Every time I start to slip into sadness about you, someone pulls me back by reassuring me of your unconditional love that was given to me every minute of every day. I pray with all of my heart that you know how much I love you, and how much I loved you back then. I know I was only four years old, but I do have some vague memories of you that will forever be in my heart. I remember going to my first Mets game. I have a picture of us there; I remember being jubilant and comforted knowing that you were next to me.

I'm a Knicks fan, just like you. I play basketball now, and during games I think about you and how you used to coach me in my Little League sports. I've also taken up another sport you loved: skiing. Even though I have had accomplishments, my best skiing memory was last year. I went down into the basement to put away my ski boots, and Great-Uncle Richie was there. He called me over and told me that not only was he proud of me, but that he saw you in me, and he promised that if you were here you would be proud of me, too. I can't begin to tell you how much that meant to me. People tell me stuff like that all the time, but coming from someone who has known you since you were born, and someone who knew how much you loved skiing, it just felt amazing. I felt your hand on my shoulder that day as if to congratulate me, and that night I went to bed crying with happiness.

There are so many things I wish I got to experience with you,

like my summers in Breezy Point. Breezy was always very dear to your heart and I have heard countless stories of you playing practical jokes on people or just telling jokes to make everyone laugh.

Dad, I can't begin to tell you how much I love you, but I hope that this letter helps you understand. I know that you are with me at all times, watching me and helping me make good choices, but every time I think of you, sadness creeps inside of my heart. I know we will not be reunited for a long time, yet I can't wait until we are. My life is great and the whole family is doing well, but we all miss you greatly.

I know this is not goodbye. This is me saying that I'll be with you some day. I miss you and I think of you with every breath I take, every word I speak, every ball I shoot and every trail I ski. I know you are always with me, and that even though our time together was short, I wouldn't have changed a minute of it. Thank you for all you've done for me. I promise to make you proud. I love you with all of my heart and soul, and I always will.

Love always,
Emma

WALTER G. HYNES

🖋

Walter Gerard Hynes was born on October 2, 1954, in New York, New York, to Walter and Margaret Hynes, and was the brother of Patricia. Walter and Veronica Fanning were married in 1987 and had three daughters, Caitlin, Kerry and Deirdre. Walter earned his BA from John Jay School of Criminal Justice and his law degree from St. John's University, and worked for the New York City Fire Department and a private law practice. He loved spending time with his wife and daughters, playing golf and family vacations. On September 11, Walter was Captain of Ladder 13 and was in the North Tower when it collapsed. He was forty-six years old.

LETTER WRITER: Ronnie Hynes (wife)
AGE: 57

Dear Walter,

Since you've been gone, there have been so many milestones with our daughters, Cait, Kerry and Deirdre. What should be joy-filled memories are filled with bittersweet moments, but I know you are still with us and you are a part of us always. You are in our hearts, and I see a special part of you in each of our girls. Each of them holds a gift that I loved about you and made you who you were, the man I fell in love with.

Ronnie, Caitlin, Walter, Kerry and Deirdre

Cait has your intelligence and is analytical and intuitive, and I know, in her future career, that she will use those gifts to help others, just as you did. Kerry has your heart and is a generous and giving young woman who shares her talents freely, helping others in need, following your example in life. And Deirdre, she has that sarcastic wit like you, which although at times seems inappropriate for her age, makes me feel like you are in the room talking to me still. It amazes me to see you in them and know that you do live on and *they are your legacy*. They are still Wally's Angels!

We are closing in on the tenth anniversary of your death and we all miss you more than ever. Sometimes it seems like one long day since we last saw you, and in other ways it seems like it was a hundred years ago. As a result of your death, we've been provided many lessons. We have been humbled by the kindness of humanity; our hearts have been overwhelmed with the love that has been showered upon us. Faith has carried us through the darkest valleys. Life, though very different from what I expected when I met you, has gone on with hope for the future when I look into the eyes of our girls. Ten years ago, I couldn't look past the moment we were living in, taking one breath at a time, needing to remind myself to breathe, and not knowing how we would live without you. Today, I look at the beautiful and strong young women whom we were blessed to teach, care for and love and I see how life has gone on and know you are with us still. Mere words can never express how much we have loved you and miss you, Walter. Your handprint is on our hearts and that can never be taken away.

Loving you always,
Ronnie

Thomas Fitzpatrick

~

Thomas James Fitzpatrick was born on October 24, 1965, in Bronx, New York, to Michael and Roseanna Fitzpatrick, and was the brother of Michael. He married Marianne Pennino in 1994 and had two children, Brendan and Caralyn. Thomas earned a BS from Boston College and an MBA from Fordham University and worked for Sandler O'Neill & Partners. He loved his children and wife, skiing and playing golf. On September 11, Thomas was at his desk on the 104th floor of the South Tower. He was thirty-five years old.

LETTER WRITER: Michael Fitzpatrick (brother)
AGE: 36

Dear my brother and best friend Thomas,
When I was only thirteen months old in October 1965, Dad and Mom brought you home and I probably wondered: "Who is this? How long is he staying? Will I love him?" Almost thirty-six years later, I knew *all* the answers. On September 11, 2001, in the prime of your life, you were called to your eternal home with God in heaven. It may not have always looked and felt like it, but I love you, my brother, from that day in October 1965 and always.

You provided me with so many wonderful memories and taught

Michael (left) and Thomas

me valuable lessons that have impacted my life.

Growing up, like most brothers close in age, we shared at first but eventually became sibling rivals. Being the second child and only one year apart, you inherited many of my clothes, my bicycle and my homework.

As siblings, we were competitive at almost everything. From basketball to bowling, from tennis to golf, in school and on and on. The competition always led us to do our best and, as you remember, the competition could sometimes get a little ugly. While it drove us, it never drove us apart. After Fordham Prep, we temporarily went our separate ways to prestigious universities, you to Boston College and I to Notre Dame. The competition was fierce then, too, but we both know who won the Liberty Bowl.

Your "just do it now" mind-set was something to be admired. You had one of the longest to-do lists I've ever seen, but crossed out items as you completed more projects than I have ever started. Only one item remained on your to-do list for a long time. After a marathon fifteen-year courtship, you finally completed your most important project and married Marianne, the love of your life.

You always wanted to be a participant and not just a spectator, whether playing golf or tennis, canoeing the Delaware, skiing the black diamonds in Vermont, or simply playing with Brendan at the park.

You not only gave others a pat on the back but also a kick in the rear, and my rear really hurt. Only a true friend can do that, and only a true friend dares to—and you dared often.

You became a successful and trusted salesman not just because you wanted to book the sale but also because you truly believed it was the right financial decision for the bank. But no matter how important work was, you made a point to get home to spend time with Marianne, Brendan and Caralyn. Since you accomplished so much by age thirty-five, I can only imagine what more you could have achieved. In spirit, you have and will continue to touch our lives and guide us through tough times and also be with us during joyful times. I know that you have and will always help us to take care of Brendan and Caralyn, and you will watch over your love, Marianne, in your own special way.

You've probably played the best golf courses in heaven, and for once you've scored par on every hole. You're still telling Boston College how they can beat Notre Dame every time.

Thomas, not a day goes by that I don't think about you and how much we all miss you. I often recall you saying one of your favorite lines: "You don't have to go home, but you can't stay here!" Life has continued to move forward but our lives have never been the same since September 11, 2001. I will always share my memories and lessons I learned from you to remind us what a special person you truly were.

Love always,
Michael

TAMITHA FREEMAN

꙰

Tamitha Freeman was born on August 26, 1966, in Brooklyn, New York, to Allen and Juanita Freeman, and was the sister of Carla. Tamitha's son, Xavier, was born on February 26, 2000. Her greatest joy in life was family—especially her son—and nothing made her happier than organizing events and getting together with family and friends. For this reason she was often called a social butterfly. Tamitha earned a BA from City College of New York and was employed by Aon Corporation. On September 11, 2001, Tamitha was on the 86th floor of the South Tower. She was thirty-five years old.

LETTER WRITER: Juanita Freeman (mother)
AGE: 68

Hi Tam,

We all miss and love you so very much. We miss Tam the peacemaker, Tam the organizer and Tam the problem solver. Most of all, we miss your heartwarming smile. You are always in my thoughts; I call your name at least twice a day when I am addressing other people, especially Xavier.

Speaking of Xavier, I know that's who you want to hear about. He is great—very loveable like his mom. He is smart, does well in school, loves people and wants everyone to be happy. He looks like you, Carla and his dad. He loves his Daddy and his Grandma White very much. He and his granddad keep me in check, or at least I let them think so. I don't know which one acts more like my husband, Xavier or his granddaddy because he has picked up all of his granddaddy's habits.

I want to thank you for leaving him in my care. I guess you knew that I would need something to take me through the weeks, the months and the years—to keep me sane. Well, I've made it. You couldn't have left me a better gift. He keeps me busy, so I don't have time to brood or feel sorry for myself—but I still miss you. I'm trying to live right so that you can welcome me with your bright smile.

Love you,
Mom, Dad, Sister and
your son, Xavier

Steven B. Paterson

🦋

Steven B. Paterson was born on January 21, 1961, in Red Bank, New Jersey, to George and Kathryn Paterson, and was the brother of George, Joseph and Lois. He started his Wall Street career just after high school when someone recognized his work ethic and brought him to First Boston. He married Lisa on June 11, 1995, and had twins, Wyatt and Lucy. He adored his family, friends, sports, food and music. He worked for Cantor Fitzgerald, and on September 11, he was at his desk on the 104th floor of the North Tower. He was forty years old.

LETTER WRITER: Lisa Paterson (wife)
AGE: 40

Dear Steven,

A few days after you were so horrifically taken from Lucy, Wyatt and me, I told a reporter amidst my shock and grief, "They may have taken my husband, but they will not take my spirit." You saw that spirit in me the night we met. You knew that I had endured many losses, and you loved and nurtured that spirit.

It has been extremely challenging raising our children without you, for I know what they have lost. Having twins is exciting, fun and overwhelming. Fourteen bottles a day were needed, and it was

you—after a full day of work, then playing, feeding and bathing them with me—who made them every night. You played ball with Wyatt every day, relishing in the excitement of his talent. When his brain injury gave way to terrible symptoms, together we fought for a cure and held each other through the many harrowing moments it brought. With Lucy you listened, talked, played and guided her as you were paving the way for a beautiful relationship that she would rely on in those teen years. It was breathtaking for me to watch your interactions. You were my best friend. The only person in the world that got me and loved me like no other. With all my losses, I felt you would never leave. Having you taken so abruptly was just so cruel.

I must say that through picking up the pieces of our shattered lives, my spirit has remained intact and even become stronger. I know that you would so appreciate that I would be able to move through the grief, confronting the trauma and feeling the pain so that I could find my inner reserve of energy, fun, hope and courage. You nurtured that in me and allowed it to blossom. You believed in me. I have had no choice but to let that gift lead the way as I raise our children on my own.

I have tried to keep your spirit alive as we move through life. You are in Lucy and Wyatt, now fourteen, and they know and remember. We are doing remarkably well amidst our heartaches and have seen surprising acts of kindness and unexpected opportunities. Wyatt is heroic in how he has faced the challenges his disability presents. Lucy is so brave and strong. Just like she was when fighting for her life when she was born. She is showing talent as an artist, photographer, lacrosse and tennis player. Their twin connection is deep and true, and they are very protective of each other. We finally got the beach house that you and I dreamed of, and it is there we feel close to you and have developed rich and great times. You would get such a kick out of the fact that I had a reading of my full-length play in NYC and got a short play produced. I am returning to my career as a school counselor. I am going to do something extraordinary for children.

I am so open to all the great possibilities life offers. Lucy, Wyatt and I hold that spirit and wake each morning with the curiosity of what the day will bring.

I love you always,
Lisa

COLLEEN DELOUGHERY

🌿

Colleen Ann Deloughery was born on June 4, 1960, in Bayonne, New Jersey, to Joseph and Sharon McNulty, and was the sister of Pat, Donna, Joe, Kevin, Jimmy, Michael and Kenny. She married Michael (Jay) Deloughery in 1991 and had two children, Amanda and Michael. In addition to her family, Colleen loved spending time in her backyard with her menagerie of nieces, nephews, cousins, circus of friends and coworkers. On September 11, Colleen worked at Aon on the 99th floor of the South Tower. She was forty-one years old.

LETTER WRITER: Pat Marrese (sister)
AGE: 43

Dear Colleen,

Not a day goes by when I don't think of you. I miss my day-to-day person, the one who knew all my secrets, my trusted confidante, my best friend. So many good memories we shared, but more importantly, you were always with me through difficult times. Open, spontaneous, generous. You laughed a lot and I teased you because you said "I love you" too much! What I would give to hear you say those words one more time. The room filled with energy when you walked in. Our rooms haven't been the same without you.

You must be so proud of your family. Jay, Amanda and Michael are amazing. Jay has done a great job with the kids. His grief just about consumed him, yet he knew the task of parenting a five-year-old and eight-year-old rested with him. Remember the picture of you with your hand pointed outward? It was from the surprise birthday party we threw for you. For Jay, that picture became you pointing to him saying, "It's up to you now."

When Amanda was about nine, she shared with me a struggle she was feeling as a result of something she heard in religion class. Her teacher talked about the importance of loving your neighbor, turning the other cheek and forgiveness. Amanda asked me how she could ever forgive the people who killed her mom. I was at a loss for the words that would make her understand and feel better. After just a few seconds, she said to me, "I guess I have to forgive these people, if not I will hate them. If I hate, I am just like them." I was blown away! This nine-year-old taught me the real lessons of forgiveness and acceptance. I don't know why I was so surprised; you lived your life that way. You seemed to understand the most tortured souls, the lonely, the hungry, were most in need of your love, and you freely gave it.

As I watch Amanda grow, I know that her compassion, sense of self, courage, determination and commitment to doing the right thing are gifts from you. She is an amazingly strong and talented young woman who seems to have a knack for making each day an adventure, and she fills her days with kindness and appreciation. Just like you, Michael is a chatterbox and social butterfly. He has not retreated from life or hid behind any walls. Michael is open to new experiences. He shows us how to be innocent, how to enjoy the small things in life, how to be carefree, how to have fun. After all they have been through, Jay, Amanda and Michael deserve the best that the world can give, and if you have anything to do with it, I know they will receive it.

Life goes on and we still wonder about why you are gone. We feel your love as you guide us to happiness and cry with us in sadness.

We know you are still with us. You will forever be in our hearts.

Love,
Patty

Pat (left) and Colleen

JASON D. CAYNE

꽃

Jason "Jake" David Cayne was born on November 11, 1968, in Manalapan, New Jersey, to Jordan and Suzan Cayne. He married Gina in 1992 and had three daughters, Suzann, Marissa and Raquel. Jake went to Kean University and worked for Cantor Fitzgerald. He loved his children, wife, parents and sister more than anything. On September 11, Jason was at his desk on the 104th floor of the North Tower. He was thirty-two years old.

LETTER WRITER: Suzann Cayne (daughter)
AGE: 17

Dear Dad,

I remember you. Everything about you. But one memory in particular keeps coming back to me: our tea parties. We would share make-believe cups of tea, put on the radio and slow dance to songs and laugh until Mom called us to dinner.

After you were gone, I couldn't stop from continuing our special tea parties.

Sitting at a small table, I pick up a pastel-colored teapot and pour a steaming cup of tea into the cup across from me. I flip my brown hair from my shoulders and straighten the plate in front of me.

"Don't forget to blow on your tea, Daddy," I warn you. "It's steamin' hot," I say as I daintily place a napkin across my lap.

I take a bite from a warm chocolate chip cookie.

"Daddy, you must try this cookie. It's probably the best food I've ever tried," I exclaim as I put one onto your plate.

As soon as I finish cleaning the mess, I stand up and walk over to the radio on my desk.

"Daddy, what song would you like to listen to?"

I flash a smile, pulling out a Spice Girls album.

I click the button and choose track number three. As the song filters through the room, I begin rocking my head back and forth in time to the rhythm of the music.

"Wow, Daddy, we have the same taste in music."

Dancing in circles, getting dizzy, I somehow end up at your chair. Looking, I give you a huge kiss on the cheek and I whisper, "Thank you for being the best Daddy in the world."

I stand up and extend my hands toward you, dancing around and around.

"Daddy, I love dancing with you. Do you like dancing with me?"

Off I twirl.

"Oh, you don't need to answer because I already know the answer," I giggle.

"Of course you love dancing with me because I am your princess."

"Daddy, this was a lot of fun, but I think it is time for dinner," I say as I start to clean everything up. "Aren't you going to help me?"

After everything is cleaned up, I make my way to the mirror that is hanging on the wall above my dresser. As I look at my reflection, not only do I see myself, but I see my father as well. I move my hands across my eyes and say, "Daddy, look, we have the same eye color! A lot of people don't like brown eyes, but I think they are very pretty. Don't you?"

I move my hands from my eyes to my hair. I examine the deep brown color.

"Daddy, we even have the same hair color!"

"Daddy, when I look into the mirror, I don't see Suzann, I see you. It's like I'm looking at a picture of you, just in girl form. It's so weird."

I move my eyes away from the mirror and glance at the cracked picture frame that is standing on my dresser. I hold the picture of my father and me that we took at the father-daughter dance.

"I miss you, Daddy. I wish that you were really here so we can have real tea parties together. I am getting tired of always having to play with my imaginary father. Whenever I talk to you, you never answer back.

"I miss the way you would tuck me in at night and the way you would tickle me. I even miss the way we would brush our teeth together and the times we would go to the park with the family. It's not fair that the only way I can really see you is when I look at a reflection of myself. I miss you so much.

"Daddy, I almost forgot to tell you that I am making so many new friends in school this year. I really like all of them and I think you would like them, too. Sometimes, I even have tea parties with them when we have sleepovers. I am also playing soccer this year, and I have been scoring so many goals. I think you would be very proud of me. Oh my gosh! I cannot believe I almost forgot to tell you that I saw a musical on Broadway! It was so good; I loved all the music they sang! This year has been a really good year. Of course I still really miss you, but I have actually been having a lot of fun."

"Suzann, come down for dinner now," Mom shouts from the bottom of the stairs. I take the picture from the frame, fold it up and place it in my pocket as I head downstairs for supper.

I miss you so much, Dad.

Love,
Your Suzy Q

Jupiter Yambem

🖎

Jupiter Yambem was born on November 4, 1959, in Imphal, Manipur, India, to Dr. Satiabati Devi Yambem and Tombi Singh, and had four brothers, Sanamani, Angamba, Ningthim and Laba. Jupiter attended North Point (Darjeeling) and St. Joseph's College in India; he also attended SUNY New Paltz, where he met his wife, Nancy McCardle, in 1981. They were married in 1991 and had one son, Santi. Jupiter enjoyed his life with a diverse group of friends and his American "family." He was founder of the North American Manipur Association, he loved the outdoors (hiking, biking, skiing and sailing) and he celebrated the everyday joys that come with being a success in America. What he enjoyed most in his short life was being a father. Jupiter worked at Windows on the World in the North Tower as a Banquet Manager, and was responsible for a daylong business meeting on September 11. He was forty-one years old.

LETTER WRITER: Nancy Yambem (wife)
AGE: 50

To My Dear "Nungshiba" (Jupiter),
I'd like to say how much we miss you, but I believe you know that. You see, I'm not sure where your soul is . . . if it is in a heavenly

place, or if it has been reincarnated into another amazing being. What I do believe is that, somehow, a part of you is still with us, that you are guiding us in how to live our lives and that you have some unworldly input into what is truly important in our lives. When I was hurting the most, I heard you say, "I'm with you."

You left an amazing mark on the world, my love. Anyone who knew you could never forget how kind you were and how genuinely and fully you lived your life. You loved being alive, celebrating everyday experiences with friends and family: cooking, eating, dancing, laughing, having a glass of good scotch or wine with friends.

The one thing that was most important to you, my love, I know, was our son, "Pa-gi Chingli" (Santi). You loved him with a passion. He misses you so very much. He is fourteen now, very different from the five-year-old you left behind.

There are so many times when tears come to my eyes . . . because I know you would have loved to see him do everything he was

meant to do in his life. You were so very proud of him, so very proud to be his father. You should be here.

Our life has changed dramatically since you've been gone, my love. We moved from our first home that you were so proud of, to the neighborhood that we dreamed of raising Santi in together; I was remarried about four years ago. (You would like Jerry . . . you never disliked anyone!)

We still miss you and love you so very much. Santi used to say, "I love you, Pa-Pa, and I always will" every night before he went to sleep. He is too old now for me to tuck him in, but I believe he still says it in his heart. I believe that is where you are, my love . . . you're with us in his—and my—heart. And that's where you will always be.

With our love always,
Your "Nungshibi"
(Nancy) and "Pa-gi
Chingli" (Santi)

JOHN RODAK

༗

John Michael Rodak was born on September 29, 1961, in Wilkes-Barre, Pennsylvania, to John J. and Regina Rodak. He married Joyce Kenish in 1986 and had two daughters, Chelsea Nicole and Devon Marie. John earned his bachelor's degree in Business Administration from LaSalle University in Philadelphia, class of 1983. His passions in life started with his daughters and wife and included fishing, golfing and hunting. On September 11, John was at his desk on the 104th floor of the South Tower working for Sandler O'Neill & Partners. He was thirty-nine years old.

LETTER WRITER: Devon Rodak (daughter)
AGE: 14

Dear Daddy,

It feels like only yesterday we were making dinner for the family. Happy as can be, smiles on our faces, laughter filling the room. But we were unaware of what the Tuesday of September 11 had in store for us. I didn't know that that Monday night would be the last time I saw your face and heard your voice and the last time I would be held in your arms.

I remember on the 11th, you called Mommy saying you were okay. I asked to talk to you but I was told you had to go. I didn't

know what was going on; I was only five. I thought you would be home any second but days, weeks, months and years have passed and it looks like my thoughts as a five-year-old were wrong. I still dream that you will walk through the door, arms open, ready to be hugged, and I even dream that you have been in the hospital for ten years. But that's too good to be true.

I cannot believe you're gone; it doesn't seem real. I talk to you often when I have problems, need help, or just need to be listened to. Every time I talk to you, I know you are listening. I feel you there. I know it sounds crazy but it's true. And when I look at the clock it's 9:11 a.m. or 9:11 p.m., and when your favorite songs come on, I know your spirit is always with me.

Our memories are still with me. The trips on the boat *The Undecided*, watching Scooby Doo, *Jaws*, *A League of Their Own*, trips to the shore and Disney World, going to North Carolina searching for wild horses but only finding their poop. Mommy told me that when I was two I would sit on the couch and cry, and in response to your asking me what was wrong, I would reply, "I want to remember Daddy." Did I know this would happen?

Daddy, I love you and I miss you.

Remember you were not just a dad to me, you were a hero. I love you like crazy.

Devon

WEIBIN WANG

⚘

Weibin Wang was born on June 14, 1960, in Guilin, China, to Zhengjie Wang and Manyu Zhang. He married Wen Shi on April 30, 1986, and had three children, Raymond, Marina and Richard. Weibin graduated from Wuhan University, China, with a BA in Physics, earned his MA in Geophysics from the University of Science and Technology of China, and earned his PhD in Geophysics from Columbia University. Dr. Wang shifted to Computer Science in 1994 and worked as a Senior Programmer/Analyst for Knight-Ridder Financial, Lehman Brothers and Cantor Fitzgerald successively. He deemed his wife and three beautiful children as important as his own life. In his spare time, Dr. Wang enjoyed golfing, volleyball, basketball, swimming, table tennis, cooking and traveling. On September 11, 2001, Dr. Wang was at his desk on the 103rd floor of the North Tower. He was forty-one years old.

LETTER WRITER: Richard Wang (son)
AGE: 12

Dear Dad,
Time really flies. The past ten years went by like a blur. Every day we miss you, Dad, and especially on September 11. Every year we go to Ground Zero to remember you on that day. Although the two

towers are gone, they are working very hard to build four new towers in their place. It tells the world that we will never forget the day and we are strong. The destruction of the Twin Towers will not defeat us. We, the American people, will stand stronger and taller even after the tragic events of 9/11/01.

So far, I am doing very well in school. This year, I entered sixth grade, and my grades are excellent. Science is my favorite subject. I want to follow in your footsteps to be a smart, successful person. When I grow up, I want to become a scientist and an inventor just like you. I would love to explore eternal life and force fields. I hope to develop a cure for humans to stay young and healthy. I hope to move on with my life, get into a good college and be successful in the future.

Dad, I love you and miss you. Over the years, I get to know more and more about you from Mom and my brother and sister. I feel so proud of having such a wonderful Dad like you. I will try my best to continue the spirit and legacy you left behind. With your beautiful memories, we will move forward to a bright and promising future.

You will live in our hearts forever. Rest in peace.

Love you,
Richard

PAUL MITCHELL

Paul Thomas Mitchell was born on July 17, 1955, in Brooklyn, New York, to George and Rosemary Mitchell, and had two sisters, Marie and Susan. After moving to Staten Island, he met and married Maureen Brown and had two daughters, Jennifer and Christine. Paul was promoted to Lieutenant with the Fire Department of New York about a year before September 11. He also coached golf, basketball and Little League soccer, collected books on the history of firefighting, grew a vegetable garden in the backyard and was a mentor and friend to many. He vacationed in Cape Cod and hoped to move there when he retired. On September 11, Paul was on his way home from a shift in Manhattan, but grabbed some gear from his previous firehouse, Hook and Ladder 110 in Brooklyn, and responded to the World Trade Center. He was forty-six years old.

LETTER WRITER: Marie Mitchell (sister)
AGE: 58

Dear Paul,
Mom died yesterday. It wasn't a surprise. The stroke she had this past July, around your birthday, took the wind out of her sails. She tried to recuperate, but then a second episode took her under the

wave. But really, she died of a broken heart. Losing you on 9/11 was something so huge and incomprehensible that even with all of her faith, resilience and "stubborn Irish," there was a void that couldn't be filled. Somehow, though, I think you already know.

It has been a long ten years since you evaporated into the enormous dust clouds at the World Trade Center site as the building collapsed. You were last seen carrying a ton of gear and heading into the South Tower, intent on rescuing folks trapped in an elevator. But no one really knows exactly where so many of New York's Bravest were that day. I was in California and had started to meditate at 5:45 a.m., which was 8:45 a.m. Eastern time, right when the first plane hit the North Tower. When I got to work and heard what had happened, I "knew" you were gone.

It took about a week to be able to fly back east. When I arrived in New York, I attended a prayer vigil at Yankee Stadium, organized by Mayor Giuliani. While we all prayed, the National Guard and Coast Guard watched over us. Afterwards, I went with a friend to the site. A firefighter from a station near yours walked me into the rubble, as far as we could go without our shoes melting. A few other firefighters emerged out of the smoke, and one of them commandeered a cherry picker to take the flowers I brought up over the pile and toss them in to you. We all hugged and cried. So much tenderness in the midst of so much horror.

I have found a lot of comfort working and training with a Community Emergency Response Team (CERT). Your story always comes up, and it has helped so many people.

I'm shuffling off to Buffalo in a few days for Mom's funeral. I know you will be there, too. I love you bunches, always have and always will. Thanks for your courage and your persistence in living the life you so wanted to live, and for excelling at what you did, both inside and outside of the fire department.

Take good care of Mom. Give her a hug for me, okay?

Marie

CRAIG WILLIAM STAUB

༚

Craig William Staub was born on September 22, 1970, in Bronx, New York, to Florence Staub, and was the brother of Barbara, Carolyn and Kenny. He graduated from Boston University summa cum laude in 1992. Craig met his true love, Stacey, in 1994 and married her on June 25, 2000. A little girl, Juliette-Craig, named for her father, came just eleven days after the attack, on his birthday. Craig was a Senior Vice President for Keefe, Bruyette & Woods and frequently did live telecasts for WebFN. He loved his family and lifelong friends, was an avid reader and loved traveling, listening to Pearl Jam, hanging with his buddies and cuddling with his wife and cat, Chewy. Though he lived in New Jersey for a year before he died, Craig was a true New Yorker born and raised. On September 11, Craig was on the 89th floor of the South Tower. He was thirty years old.

LETTER WRITER: Stacey Staub (wife)
AGE: 40

Dear Craig,
We were often told that we had the kind of love most people search for but few ever find. A love that was born out of true friendship and filled with mutual respect, constant laughter, warm compas-

sion, life's daily compromises and challenges, and a lot of passion. When friends asked you for advice on finding their one true love, you always said, "Make sure that the person you find is your best friend. Stacey is my best friend—I wouldn't want to be anywhere or do anything without her." And you spent our time together showering me with affection, making me smile and creating so many memories for me to treasure. Older married couples have commented that we packed more into seven years than they have in more than twenty. Though we were only blessed with a short time together, I have no regrets, for we spent that time enjoying life and, more importantly, enjoying each other. You will always be my greatest friend.

Craig, I know in my heart that you are here with me right now. How could you not be?

The gift I had made for you for our wedding—the framed and hand-calligraphy letter describing my love for you—still resonates with me. You know, an excerpt from the book *The Notebook* by Nicholas Sparks:

> *Every day we are together*
> *Is the greatest day of my life.*
> *I will always be yours.*

Craig, I would like to thank you. Not only for loving me so deeply and unconditionally but also for leaving me with your greatest, most precious and generous gift of all—your child, Juliette-Craig. It warms my heart to look at her and see you looking back at me. And when she came into this world on your birthday, I knew that September 22 was meant to always be a happy day, a special day. That day will always be a celebration of her life and yours.

I promise to spend the rest of my life raising our daughter and loving her enough for the both of us. I will strive to make you proud of me and of her. And she will always know that her daddy in heaven was the greatest man that ever lived. You will be missed every moment of every day. I will always love you . . . my heart is yours.

Love,
Stacey

Brooke Alexandra Jackman

꘡

Brooke Alexandra Jackman was born on August 28, 1978, in Oyster Bay, New York, to Robert and Barbara Jackman, and had two older siblings, Erin and Ross. Brooke graduated from Columbia University with a BA in History and Women's Studies and was working on the Agency desk at Cantor Fitzgerald on the 104th floor of the North Tower. She loved to read, party, be with her friends and family, dance, play music and ski. Brooke was in the process of applying to graduate school for social work to fulfill her dream of working with underprivileged children. She was twenty-three years old.

LETTER WRITER: Barbara Jackman (mother)
AGE: 65

Dearest Brooke,

I can hardly believe that ten years have passed without having you in our lives. We have had two additions to our family—you would love your two little nieces, Blake Ava and Elle Olivia. Blake loves to hear stories about the aunt that she is named for—it makes her feel so special. I tell her about your beautiful brown eyes, your dancing smile, your great sense of style, your courage, your determination and your tremendous heart. I tell her that we only had twenty-three years with you, but the joy that you brought to our family will last forever. Not a day goes by that we don't think of you and miss you. Elle loves her books. I tell her that from the time you were a little girl, books were your passion, and you read almost a book a day. You would be reading as you got off the school bus, at camp with a flashlight under the covers when you were supposed to be sleeping and as a young adult walking down the city streets.

You had an incredible mind with total recall. If we asked you about something that happened ten years ago, you would be able to tell us the date, the time, the people present and even what we were wearing. We remember your graduation from Columbia University and how proud we were of you. We knew that our adorable little girl had become a beautiful young woman who was independent and full of life. You were someone who always spoke her mind while never accepting prejudice, stereotypes or discrimination. You saw the best in everyone. You didn't like wastefulness or dishonesty. To your friends, you were the person who got the inside joke, who gave the best advice and who was trusted enough to be a special confidante. Although you were so many different things to so many people, one thing that everyone knew was that they could count on Brooke.

Blake and Elle know all about the Brooke Jackman Foundation that was started to embody your spirit and to carry out your dreams. You would be so proud to see how many at-risk children will have a chance in this world because of you. We were all blessed to have you in our lives. Erin misses her shopping partner and fix-it person, but most of all she misses her sister, her best friend. Ross misses the little sister he would quiz on sports, and his best little buddy. For Iris, you were the little sister she never had. Daddy misses his little baby, the Brookster, and I miss the light of my life. To the rest of the family you were a precious young woman with a heart of gold. You will forever be treasured and loved by all who knew you.

We love you,
Mommy

DOUGLAS GURIAN

꜖

Douglas Gurian was born on July 6, 1963, in New York, New York, the only child of Bruce and Marie Gurian. He lived most of his life in and around New York City and Englewood, New Jersey. He graduated from the U.S. Military Academy at West Point in 1986. After serving in the army in Germany for several years, he returned to New York in 1990 where he met his wife, Susan. They were married in 1992. Their son, Tyler, was born in 1994 and their daughter, Eva, was born in 1997. At the time of his death, Douglas was living in Tenafly, New Jersey, with his wife and children. He worked at Radianz and on 9/11 was attending a technology show at Windows on the World in the North Tower. He was thirty-eight years old.

LETTER WRITER: Eva Gurian (daughter)
AGE: 13

Dear Daddy,

Growing up without a father is the hardest thing I'll ever have to do. On September 11, 2001, families and individuals across America were deeply saddened by the loss of family members and friends. I was one of those people. That day, you were on the 110th floor of the North Tower in the World Trade Center. You left for work that morning and you never came home.

September 11, 2001, began as any other typical morning, or so I thought. Tyler and I woke up very early in the morning, so you got up and lay down next to us to put us back to sleep. You and Mom tried as usual to leave quietly for work. Once again, the car engine awakened me. You watched my window slide open and saw me stick my head out and yell, "Bye, Mommy! Bye, Daddy!" I waved at you and you happily waved back. I didn't know it yet, but when you pulled out of the driveway that morning, it would be the last time I would ever see you.

During the school day, my teacher told me that my babysitter was here to pick me up. Tyler was already in the car and my baby-sitter looked worried. I never would have guessed what had really happened. We arrived home and waited a while. Mom had told my babysitter to not let us turn on the TV. Soon, Mom came home with two men who had driven her back from New York. I sat on the stairs when Mom opened the door, her face filled with tears. Mom sat with Tyler and me on the stairs and told us that a terrible thing had happened.

The road of my life before was a peaceful street. However, it eventually came to a dead end and I couldn't find another path to take. I walked across a field of memories and came to a busy highway full of excitement and opportunities. I keep going on that highway every day, but I know that no matter how far I go, I'll never come to an exit ramp back to the first four years of my life. I know I can always look back at that field of memories.

I think about you every day and miss you immensely. We have pictures of you, your watch, your towel, and your clothes. My favorite memory is Fire Island, the place where you grew up and where you made friends that our family is still friends with today. I go to Fire Island all the time, watching the waves that you used to swim in and where your ashes are scattered in places that you once were. I am surrounded by your love everywhere, and whenever the wind carrying my grief hits me, knowing that you love me gives me that extra push I need to keep going, to keep smiling. I know that your memory lives on and it will forever.

Love,
Eva

HOWARD SELWYN

Howard Selwyn was born on August 2, 1954, in Leeds, England, to Leslie and Norma Selwyn, and was the brother of Russell, Ian and Lisa. He married Frances Ruth Levin in 1979, and they moved from London to New York a year later. Howard was the father of two sons, James and Alexander. He loved coaching soccer for both boys and also played goalkeeper for an over-forty team. He continued to follow his favorite English soccer team, Leeds United, and would watch them even if the only broadcast available was in Spanish. On September 11, 2001, Howard was at his desk on the 84th floor of the South Tower. He was forty-seven years old.

LETTER WRITER: James Selwyn (son)
AGE: 29

Dear Dad,
You worked for Euro Brokers in the fixed-dates money market. This is how the typical conversation went.
"What do you do for a living?"
"I am a money broker."
"A what? Is that like a stockbroker?"
"Not in the slightest bit."
The Q and A would go on for several minutes and at the end of the conversation, they still didn't know what you did. The truth is,

to this day, I still do not fully understand what you did every day, despite having a degree in Finance and working as a trader in the futures market.

I realized after having my first child last year that it is important for her to one day understand why her grandfather was on the 84th floor of 2 World Trade Center on that Tuesday morning in September. Your job in that building made a huge impact on my life and is the reason that my job is what it is today.

You and Mom were both transplanted New Yorkers, both born and raised in England. When you left England in late 1980, no one could have imagined that in less than a year, New York would become your permanent home.

I'll never forget visiting your WTC office. The day would always begin very early, 4:00 a.m. to be exact, the time your alarm would go off every morning. We would leave the house in darkness with travel mugs full of English breakfast tea.

Each year, it would always be the same, and that is what stuck with me: the sounds, the smells, and the faces of your colleagues.

When I hear athletes talk about going to ballgames with their fathers and deciding that they wanted to play one day when they got older, I know exactly how they must have felt. Each year, when you brought me to the World Trade Center and I saw the financial markets up close, I knew that I wanted to be a part of it.

Just writing this now makes me realize how lucky I was to have such an amazing father. Even though you were up so early for work, you still managed to coach our soccer teams, help with school work, take me to ballgames, etc. I'll never forget how happy you were when I went to the University at Buffalo to study business. The last time I saw you, you helped me move into an off-campus apartment as I started my sophomore year. I was able to see how excited it made you to see me having such a great college experience, as school simply wasn't like this when you were growing up in England.

I think about my everyday life and realize how much I learned from you and what an impact you have had on me. I work in the World Financial Center and have walked past the WTC site every day for the last six years. I'm often asked if that is difficult for me. The truth is that it has become somewhat comforting over time. I know that every day I will think about you and all the good memories I have from growing up.

As a new parent now myself, I know what it takes to be a great father because I am lucky enough to have had the best one.

In loving memory of HS & FRS

Your loving
and grateful son,
James

VINCENT HALLORAN

꜒

Vincent Gerard Halloran was born on July 31, 1958, in Flushing, New York, to Joseph and Mary Alice Halloran, and he was the brother of Maureen, Terence, Patricia and James. He married Marie Parkanzky on May 17, 1986, and had six children, Jake, Conor, Aidan, Kieran, Declan and Phelan, who was born on their sixteenth wedding anniversary, eight months after 9/11. Vincent worked as a firefighter at Engine 262, Ladder 43, and then as Lieutenant at Ladder 8 where he celebrated twenty years on the job on September 5, 2001. While he loved his job, working with the guys and helping others, nothing was as important to him as his family. On September 11, 2001, Vincent was lost in the lobby of the North Tower after leading all of his men to safety. He was forty-three years old.

LETTER WRITER: Marie Halloran (wife)
AGE: 41

Dear Vince,
In 2001, we were a happy family of seven. We had just finished a wonderful summer with the kids. Little did we know that in a blink of an eye, you would be gone and I would be left to raise our children alone.

About two months after we lost you, I learned that I was pregnant with our only daughter, and my due date was our sixteenth wedding anniversary. I really felt that you had given me one last precious gift from heaven. You always put so much thought and care into choosing the perfect gift and this one couldn't have been better.

We held your memorial at St. Patrick's Cathedral on November 9, 2001. I was told that the cathedral holds five thousand people. For you, it was standing-room only with many others standing outside. The boys' altar served and Cardinal Egan presided. The gathering truly reaffirmed how special you are. Your friends told wonderful stories about you and an announcement was made about the new addition to our family. Nothing like sharing news with more than five thousand of our closest friends. Tears come to my eyes when I think of all that you have missed, from the birth of your beautiful daughter—our youngest child—to Communions, acceptances to private high school for two of the boys, graduations from high school and college, acceptances to graduate schools and even the start of careers.

Jake is now twenty-five and working full-time—he is so hard-working like you.

Conor is working on his master's—he is so compassionate like you.

Aidan just graduated from college—he is so friendly like you.

Kieran just started college—he is so funny like you.

Declan is in middle school—can you believe it?—he is so energetic like you.

Phelan is your precious gift to us—she is so witty like you.

As for me, I tried becoming a consultant for a while and then decided to focus on my most precious possessions—our children. I am happy with that decision and have made as full a life as possible with new friends and experiences.

All of us who love you are now proud to remember your life. The havoc you wreaked as a child. How you once gave a stranger with a flat your own spare tire and actually got it back. How you refused to celebrate Valentine's Day but brought me flowers every week of our marriage. How you ran the house like a camp—Camp Halloran, as you called it, taking the boys bike riding, kayaking, camping, shaping them into the men they are today. How you loved the firehouse life, turning the roof into a thriving greenhouse and mentoring the younger guys. And, on September 11, how you helped evacuate the North Tower, turned everyone around on the 30th floor when you smelled jet fuel, shouted to the others to leave once you reached the lobby, then disappeared.

I appreciate every minute that we had together. I am pleased to let you know that some of your wonderful traits have transferred to me and I am a more patient, caring, loving, and easygoing person. The kids might think differently, but I know it. I love you and always will.

Marie

MICHAEL J. PASCUMA JR.

Michael J. Pascuma Jr. was born on January 8, 1951, in Richmond Hill, New York, to Michael Sr. and Ada Pascuma. He married Linda in 1974 and had three children, Melissa, Michael and Christopher. He worked as a stockbroker on the American Stock Exchange. He loved spending time with his wife and children. He loved golf, playing blackjack and just enjoying life. On September 11, 2001, Michael was at a breakfast meeting at Windows on the World in the North Tower. He was fifty years old.

LETTER WRITER: Melissa Pascuma-Gangi (daughter)
AGE: 33

Dear Daddy,

Ten years ago I was forced into a life that I didn't want and never expected. The pain is still so strong and it is still so hard to wrap my mind around the tragedy that happened in our world, our country, our state, our family. Can you see and feel my pain, Daddy? Do you know how much I love and miss you? The sadness in my heart will never go away and when I think of, or see the images of, that day it is hard for me to breathe. When I saw that tall, strong tower crumble to the ground, my happiness went with it.

The anger and sadness that I felt was then, and still is now, indescribable. I could not believe this could happen. How? Why? You were the kindest, most generous person I knew. You were so full of life and love. I felt the safest when I was with you.

Part of my heart came back when my beautiful girls were born. Madison Michael (named after my hero) in 2005 and Ella Paige in 2009. They have allowed me to smile and live again. I think of you often and imagine a life with you in it.

I imagine you walking me down the aisle and handing me to Pete and then us having our father-daughter dance.

I imagine big family dinners that you generously take us out for and laughing because you just told one of your jokes so perfectly.

I imagine on sunny beautiful weekends you playing golf with your friends and going to Tobay Beach with Mommy, Michael, Christopher and me. You spend a half hour carefully applying several different suntan lotions to get the perfect tan.

I imagine my girls thinking you are just hysterical. Madison would love your silliness and ask, "When is Grandpa coming over?"

I imagine us going on big Disney vacations and you spoiling Madison and Ella. You would want to go golfing or lie in the sun instead of going to the theme parks and Madison would say, "Please, Grandpa, come with us on rides." And you would.

I imagine my life as it was on 9/10/01 . . .

As the years without you continue to pass, I can't help but feel like I am forgetting you and our memories are fading. It breaks my heart. But your five-year-old granddaughter taught me an important lesson. Pete (her daddy) had been commuting into the city, and as we passed the train station one day, Madison asked me if this is where her daddy leaves to get to the city. I told her yes. She then started yelling, "Hi, Daddy. I love you, Daddy. I miss you. See you when you get home!" I laughed and said, "Madison, Daddy can't hear you. He is in the city." And in her five-year-old, I-know-everything-and-you-know-nothing voice she said, "Mom, me and Daddy have a love path. It doesn't matter where we are. I can be at school, camp or at home and me and Daddy can send messages back and forth through our love path." She taught me something that day that I had forgotten. I needed to start using our "love path" so that I can feel close to you again. Because it doesn't matter where you are and where I am. No one can take away the special memories, relationship and love we will always have for each other.

Daddy, I love and miss you today, tomorrow and forever.

Love you endlessly,
Your daughter,
Melissa Pascuma-
Gangi

WILLIAM RALPH RAUB

🌿

William Ralph Raub was born on January 9, 1963, in Suffern, New York, to Stan and Annette Raub, and he was the brother of Susan and Marie. He grew up in Delmar, New York. He married Maureen Jeffers in 1991 and had two children, Rebecca, born in 1995, and Liam, born in June of 2001. Will graduated summa cum laude from Siena College, where he earned a BS in Finance. He worked at Cantor Fitzgerald and was Senior Vice President, Institutional Equity Sales as well as a Partner. Will was a serious wine collector and enjoyed traveling, hosting holidays and dinner parties, and playing golf. He especially enjoyed teaching his young daughter how to play golf and hoped to do the same with his son. He was also very charitable and was passionate about helping others, especially those in need. On September 11, Will was on the 104th floor of the North Tower, on the phone with a client working in the Pan Am building, who was witnessing what was happening and relaying what he saw to Will. He was thirty-eight years old.

LETTER WRITER: Maureen Raub (wife)
AGE: 50

Dear Will,

I want to write this letter to you as an expression of my deep gratitude and appreciation for the person you were and for all that you

did. I feel so lucky to have met you, married you and shared with you the thirteen years that we had together. I will fondly look back on the wonderful memories and will always be grateful that you were a part of my life. You were beautiful in every way. You were an amazing man, an awesome husband and fantastic father. Rebecca, Liam and I were very blessed to have had you!

You had a deep sense of obligation to whatever relationship, project or job you were involved in and, as a result, you were so respected and adored by everyone who knew you. Your heart was big, and you touched so many people with it. It seemed there was a heart connection in all that you did, and from that flowed abundance and love. Thank you for setting such a positive example and bringing that energy into our lives.

Your family and friends continue to miss you, but your children miss you especially. We created two phenomenal human beings—I'm sure you know that! Rebecca is now sixteen. She has so many of your traits. She's very ambitious, very intelligent and very successful, beautiful on the inside and outside, and what a wonderful mind she has. I am hoping that she and her generation of smart, compassionate, action-oriented peace seekers will become the new leadership that will get this world on track. Liam, who is now ten, is filled with the same bright energy, smiles and light that he had when he was just three months old. His happy spirit, laughter and joy are infectious. And his timing on entering this world couldn't have been better, for he provided great comfort and healing to all of us during that awful first couple of years after 9/11.

Though this tragedy created, and still creates, great sadness for all of us, I have learned that the most important thing when faced with any challenge is how you respond to it. Dealing with all the pain, all the sorrow, all the emptiness and loss was a great challenge. I've seen others respond to tragedy and life's challenges by becoming paralyzed, depressed and overwhelmed by it. So I've tried very hard to not let these circumstances diminish my life and have come to embrace this horrible event in our lives as a catalyst for new beginnings, new possibilities and a new road to travel on.

I'm grateful to be living life more consciously and so appreciate all I have. From the bottom of my heart, I want to thank you, Will. You were a great friend and companion and you will never be forgotten. So until we meet again . . .

Love always,
Maureen

JEFFREY P. WALZ

~

Jeffrey P. Walz was born on March 29, 1964, in Staten Island, New York, to Raymond and Jennie Walz, and was the brother of Raymond and Karen. He joined the New York City Fire Department in 1993, assigned to Ladder 9. He and his wife, Rani, married in October of 1995, and welcomed their son, Bradley, in May of 1998. Jeffrey loved his family; working part-time as an electrical engineer working on aircraft carrier catapult systems for the U.S. Navy in Lakehurst, New Jersey; the New York Giants; and being a member of the FDNY. Jeff was posthumously promoted to Lieutenant shortly after 9/11. He was in the South Tower. He was thirty-seven years old.

LETTER WRITER: Karen Ciaccio (sister)
AGE: 34

Dear Jeff,

The ninth anniversary of September 11 last year was more memorable and special to me than any of the other anniversaries. How could this day be referred to as "special"? Well, your nephew Matthew, now eleven years old, came with me to Postcards. Postcards is a beautiful tribute to the all of the Staten Islanders that were ripped out of our lives that day. He wanted to read your name, and that he did . . . with pride!! Jeff, he read your name so beautifully and clear. I was so proud of him. He wore your blue FDNY work shirt; I don't know how this shirt could have fit you because it is a pretty good fit on him, and he's tall but less than a hundred pounds. Anyway, he held a photo of you, too. Having my son next to me and reading some names and a poem titled "If They Could Speak" made the anniversary a little more bearable. But I think it was the first time that Matthew has really begun to understand the magnitude of that day . . .

I still can't comprehend the magnitude of that day. It still does not seem real. There is always something missing . . . and that is you. Mommy always speaks about you, from when you were a baby until the day you died. Daddy, on the other hand, being a retired fireman himself, doesn't say as much.

I know you are getting a kick out of my girls. Lindsey's middle name is Jeffie. Right after I gave birth to her, the doctor commented on her unusual middle name. I explained that my brother, Jeffrey, was a NYC firefighter who died on 9/11 when I was four and a half months pregnant. I don't know how I made it through the rest of that pregnancy with no complications. You must have been guiding me every step of the way.

My three beautiful children, Matthew, Lindsey Jeffie, and Julia, have really been cheated in life. They never had the chance to hang out with their awesome fireman uncle.

There are two great accomplishments that have made our family extra special . . . Rani and Bradley. Your wife is awesome, and your son, Bradley (now we have to call him Brad—he is soon entering the teen years), is amazing. I truly believe you could not have left this good earth until you blessed our lives with theirs.

Love, your little sister,
Karen

Raymond, Karen and Jeff

MICHAEL STABILE

✺

Michael Stabile was born on January 11, 1951, in Brooklyn, New York, to Carl and Anna Stabile, and was the youngest of five children—Richard, John, Carol and Lucille. He married his childhood sweetheart, Roseanne Giambrone, on October 8, 1973, and had three children, Michelle, Robert and Lauren. Michael worked as a Currency Broker for Euro Brokers. Besides enjoying time with his family, Michael was deeply involved with the Catholic Youth Organization's Sports Program both as a coach and basketball referee in addition to being an avid and rabid New York Mets and Jets fan. On September 11, Michael was descending a stairwell from the 84th floor of the South Tower. He was fifty years old.

LETTER WRITER: Tony Ottomano (uncle)
AGE: 69

Dear Michael,
The word "dash" is a small, simple word. When I looked up its meaning in the dictionary, I was both surprised and amazed that the word "dash" was defined/used in no less than twenty-one ways. None of the definitions/uses aptly defined the word "dash" when I delivered your eulogy on October 7, 2001.

Michael, Jimmy (Tony's son), Tony

The dash represents the quality of one's life within the allotted time frame that has been so generously given to us. When we are born, our dash begins; when we die, our dash is completed. Our dash is the sum total of our lives—for better or for worse.

I think about your dash. The contents of your life were defined by the content of your character. Your life was personified by caring, giving, sharing and empathy. You fulfilled your responsibilities as a husband, father, son, relative and friend with purpose and determination. As I remember you, I cannot help but recall the pain and grief endured by Roseanne, Michelle, Robert and Lauren, even to this day.

It may be a bit presumptuous on my part, but knowing you, I think your message to us would be that life is a fragile, precious gift whose true essence is rooted in giving. You would advise us that our lives come with a limited warranty and an expiration. Finally, your message would remind us that we only get one chance to live our dash—live it well, be it long or short.

You were a proud American, Michael, loyal to our country and a defender of its principles. You were a devout Christian, a faithful husband, a loving father and a beloved relative and friend. You were a man of fun and laughter, and a man filled with humility.

I am reminded of Saint Augustine's description of humility:

It was pride that changed angels into devils; it is humility that makes men as angels.

Rest in peace, Michael. I am sure you are among the angels.

Love,
Uncle Tony

JEFFREY SMITH

✺

Jeffrey Randall Smith was born on April 19, 1965, in Fort Worth, Texas, to Arthur and Madeline Smith, and had two older siblings, Brenda and Jerry. He married Ellen Bakalian in 1997, and had two daughters, Margaret and Charlotte. Jeff received his BA and his MBA from the University of Rochester, where he played Division III football. He was an Equity Research Analyst for Sandler O'Neill and Partners, on the 104th floor of the South Tower. Jeff loved the Miami Hurricanes football team, scuba diving and traveling with his family. On September 11, 2001, Jeff was most likely on the Sandler trading floor, talking about the previous night's Yankees game, which he attended with daughter Maggie. He was thirty-six years old.

LETTER WRITER: Maggie and Charlotte Smith (daughters)
AGES: 12 and 10

Dear Dad,
What is it like having a dad? We wouldn't know the experience, unfortunately, because you were killed when we were so young. Our ages were two and a half and ten months old. How could that have happened to two little children? You were only our dad for a short while. It's still hard to believe that you haven't been here the

whole time. You missed birthdays, soccer games and even just ordinary dinners every night. Mom tries to play the roles of two parents, but it's just not the same. What's it like having two parents?

Having a loss is a big deal. It can ruin lives, but that's not what happened because Mom saved us. She wanted to make sure that the terrorists wouldn't ruin our lives, and she made it completely safe for us. Our lives could be full of sorrow, and we could have stopped talking about you, but it's not like that at all. We talk about you every day; you are a part of our lives. We know how you

Charlotte, Jeffrey and Maggie

would think and act; at least we think we do. Our lives aren't full of sorrow, but rather full of joy. Joy for the life you lived, not sorrow for the life you are missing.

Now we're ten and twelve. When we grow up, our goals are to become an artist/soccer player and an actress/dancer. We are trying as hard as we can to be the girls you wanted us to be, to do the things you and Mom were planning to do with us as a family.

We know you were the best dad possible. We remember that you let us help you put your tie on in the morning. You carried us up mountains in New England and into cathedral domes in Europe, and you took us to baseball games in NYC. We watched the Miami Hurricanes play football and ate barbecue wings. Life with you couldn't have been any better.

We are fortunate people in a very unfortunate way, and we know you would be proud of us. "It's all good," we say, and we "hang tuff."

Knowing that you would be proud of us helps us out a lot. It keeps us happy. The best dad on earth is proud of us. He is proudly watching over us.

> Missing you;
> loving you—
> xoxo, Maggie and
> Charlotte

STEVE POLLICINO

🖎

Steve Pollicino was born on February 2, 1953, in Brooklyn, New York, to Nick and Ann Pollicino. He married Jane Elefante in 1978, and had two children, Steven and Celeste. He grew up in Hicksville, New York, and earned a BS from Long Island University at CW Post. After starting out as a business owner, he joined the finance world and spent fifteen years working at Cantor Fitzgerald. Making the most of every minute, Steve appreciated his family and friends, and his greatest pleasure was spending time with his children. Steve managed to escape from the 104th floor during the 1993 attack, but there was no way out of the North Tower on September 11. He was forty-eight years old.

LETTER WRITER: Jane Pollicino (wife)
AGE: 57

Dear Steve,
How strange is it that I find myself writing a letter to you? I believe that the only time we ever wrote letters to each other was in 1973 and 1974 when I was away at school in Buffalo. Those days seem so long ago and sometimes it seems like they never happened; perhaps they were too good to be true. September 11 is a moment that not only changed my life but, in some ways, continues to define it.

After twenty-three years of marriage and raising two children, who would have ever thought that I would be writing to you under these circumstances? Yet writing is therapy for me, starting with the hundreds of thank-you notes that I wrote in the months and years following 9/11. I realize the value of responding from the heart and getting back to all of those friends, family members and even strangers who reached out in so many thoughtful ways.

The fact that your death, at the age of forty-eight, was part of a major, unprecedented, historic event created an unusual struggle. The families needed to rely on each other in order to muddle through the process. Believe it or not, we still continue to do so, and I count my blessings for the special people that have come into my life because of 9/11. I appreciate the unique bond that we share.

I think you would agree that our kids are carrying on with their lives in a way that we had hoped for and I thank God for that. You would be so proud of them, Steve. They were twelve and nineteen when we lost you, but your essence continues to flourish as they grow into young adults. Even with so much going on in their lives, we never stop missing you.

You missed a confirmation, graduations, proms and your son's "perfect wedding." I know that when you were lucky enough to meet Jenna in June of 2001 that you were impressed. You remember Steven and Jenna met as college freshmen at the University of Delaware? Well, in November of 2009, they became Mr. and Mrs. S. Pollicino.

And Celeste? You would have enjoyed watching her play volleyball in high school, and she has made the most out of her college years at Towson University, as she begins to finish up her degree in Graphic Design. Her hope is to live and work in the city like her brother, and I am grateful that neither of them became fearful of New York.

I feel blessed that our children are growing to be more and more like you with every passing day. Although I miss the luxury of the casual secure life we all once shared, I think that given the choice, we all feel better off having had you in our lives than if we never had you at all. It is a comfort for me to know that you made the most of every moment in your life, and that's a principle we try to live our lives by now. You appreciated what you had—I have no doubts about that.

It has been difficult, but once I came to grips with the fact that I wasn't going to put the events of 9/11 "away" and couldn't avoid it, I decided to begin volunteer work downtown, at the Tribute Center, which was established to honor your memory, along with the thousands of others whose lives were lost.

God certainly gave me, and anyone who had the pleasure and privilege of knowing you, a gift. I am most grateful and ask that He continue to bless and guide us as we continue to navigate our lives without you.

Always with love,
From Jane

PAUL JOSHUA FRIEDMAN

🕊

Paul Joshua Friedman was born on August 13, 1956, in Brooklyn, New York, to Harold and Selma Friedman, and was the brother of Iris, Amy, James and Meryl. He married Audrey Ades in 1994, and they adopted Richard Harry Hyun-Soo Friedman four months before 9/11. They called him Rocky. Paul earned a BA from Johns Hopkins University, an MSE from the University of Michigan and an MBA from New York University, and worked for Emergence Consulting in Lincoln, Massachusetts. Paul dearly loved his family, photography and nature. On September 11, he boarded American Airlines Flight 11 to travel to a management consulting project at Warner Bros. He'd delayed his trip to spend an extra day with Rocky. Paul was forty-five years old.

LETTER WRITER: Selma Friedman (mother)
AGE: 81

Dear Paul,
Sometimes I think of you as the sweet child you were, sometimes as the sweet man you became, a loving, aesthetic, knowledgeable man who still retained the visibly refreshing ability to be amazed.

I remember the way you looked the last time I saw you, when you, Audrey and baby Rocky visited from Boston. Rocky is not a baby anymore; he's ten years old. There are also three young grand-children, born within the last decade, who have swelled the Fried-man family numbers.

Paul, life does go on—it's just different in a world without you. The tragedy of September 11 has affected us in profound yet subtle ways. Priorities have changed, attitudes have been readjusted.

What will forever remain a constant is the love and respect I have felt for you, both while you were here and since you've been gone. You will always be a dear, dear son and I will always be your mom. Always.

Love,
Mom

Salvatore F. Pepe

~

Salvatore F. Pepe was born on January 29, 1956, in Bronx, New York, to Antonio and Fulvia Pepe, and was the youngest of seven children: Antonio, Genoveffa, Rosa, Anne, Leonida and Patrizia. He married Catherine Ng in 1997 and had one son, Salvatore Loong Pepe. Sal earned a BS in Industrial Engineering from Pratt University and worked for Marsh & McLennan. He loved his son, wife, extended families, astronomy, motorcycle riding, reading, traveling and keeping family relationships and traditions alive. On September 11, Sal was at his desk on the 97th floor of the North Tower. He was forty-five years old.

LETTER WRITER: Catherine Ng-Pepe (wife)
AGE: 48

Dearest Sal,

Life does go on, but it hasn't been the same without you. No one knew me better than you and no one ever will.

I always felt that you would give me a sign that it was time to take the next step, and you did. I have been waiting for your remains all these years but none have arrived. This year, with Dad and our son's involvement, we have set your headstone and buried items that reminded us of you. Our families got together to celebrate you and your life and all of the treasured memories you gave us.

Some of the items I placed in the chest: a musical hot air balloon that plays "Jingle Bells," a ponderosa pinecone from your collection, and sand from Mattituck. Each of these items brought back wonderful memories and also represented who you were.

The hot air balloon represented how special Christmas was to you and your gift to make a dream come true. The pinecone represents how you were always in awe of the natural beauty that surrounds us each day. The sand from Mattituck represents your sense of adventure, exploration and discovery.

Our son is very much like you, and I know your spirit lives on in him. Recently, for his birthday, he asked for a scrapbook of memories of you, and your family made his wish come true.

For now, our journey through this life is different from what we had expected, but I know you continue to be there by my side to guide me and our son. Our flame of love continues to burn brightly in my heart. I will always love you forever.

Cat

Barbara M. Habib

Barbara M. Habib was born on November 15, 1951, in Brooklyn, New York, to Isadore and Frances Antoci, and was the sister of George and John. She married Raymond C. Habib on June 13, 1998. Barbara earned her degree from Kingsborough Community College and became a Senior Vice President for Marsh & Mc-Lennan. She loved to cook, work in her garden and was involved with animal rights. On September 11, she was attending a meeting on the 99th floor of the North Tower. She was forty-nine years old.

LETTER WRITER: Raymond C. Habib (husband)
AGE: 59

Dear Barb,

It is hard to believe that it is almost ten years since I saw you last. I can still remember that smile on your face when you cooked our first meal in your new kitchen on September 10, having just moved into our new fully renovated apartment. Little did I know it would be our last.

I am sure you would have done the same, but I did not feel right staying in the apartment. I sold the place shortly after you left. The new furniture that you loved so much is now in the home of our good friends down the Jersey Shore.

You would be so proud of me in the new house. I actually enjoy doing the laundry and keeping the place neat and clean. Not as well as you did, but much better than years ago. You taught me well!

Fate has always been a big part of our life from our very first meeting to your last day on earth. Why did you have to be in the WTC offices of Marsh rather than your usual office in Midtown? I have stopped asking these questions and have accepted the fact that the eight great years we were together were some part of a master plan for the two of us.

Having now been put into the position of being "the husband who lost his wife on 9/11," I have chosen to accept this role but not let it define me. People want to know about you, what you were like, and that helps to keep you alive in spirit.

Your memorial service was one of pure elegance, if that is possible. It was attended by all of your family, friends and coworkers. People came from all over, many of whom I was meeting for the first time. Your brother, MaryAnn and I all spoke well about you. The Daughters of St. Paul were so helpful and they sang like the angels they are.

I have become involved with an organization called Tribute WTC, which tells the story of the World Trade Center before and after the buildings were built and destroyed. People come from all over the world, and they want to know all about you. I promise you that I do not go into too much detail, but I find it so ironic that you were one of the most private persons I had ever met, and now you are part of one of the most public events in our nation's history. Fate!

I guess it will all make sense someday, but until that time please know that I think about you every day, and know that the love we shared was a very special one and you are with me at all times.

Love always,
Ray

MICHELE LANZA

Michele Bernadette Chamberlain was born on April 26, 1965, in Staten Island, New York, to Albert A. and Ethel Chamberlain, and had older siblings Albert G. and Susan and was followed by Cynthia. Her marriage in 1990 to Robert A. Lanza Jr. produced one son, Nicholas Joshua. Michele was a fully licensed cosmetologist—credentials earned from McKee Vocational High School. She was a self-taught computer whiz, becoming an Administrative Assistant/Office Manager for Fiduciary Trust. Her hobbies included sewing, home decorating and spending much time outdoors. Her greatest love in life was her son, Nicholas—who always came first. On September 11, 2001, Michele was in her office on the 97th floor of the South Tower. She was thirty-six years old.

LETTER WRITER: Cindy Oricchio (sister)
AGE: 40

Dear Michele,

I miss you. I think you know that. It is hard to believe that it has been ten years since we lost you.

Nicholas misses his mother. He is sixteen now and, along with my three daughters, Nicollette, Jacqueline and Victoria, I think it is time they knew the real you.

You entered this world in a fury in 1965, not even waiting until Mom had a hospital room to deliver you. You were the one and only family member with blond hair and blue eyes. You stood out from the rest of us, which hinted at your uniqueness. You *were* different and you *were* special. When I was born one day after your fifth birthday, you instantly became my guardian angel. Remember when you would read books to me at night before going to bed? You

Michele (left) and Cindy

were a nurturing, compassionate and very conscientious soul from the very beginning.

I want your son and my daughters to know just how selfless you were. When you lived in Virginia and befriended a man who became quite ill with cancer, you remained by him through his illness—even in its very darkest hours. And you were there for Aunt Peggy while she battled cancer as well.

Michele, what means the most to me was just how much you loved my kids as if they were your own. Sadly, you never had the chance to meet Tori. I still laugh when I think about you referring to Jackie as "Mini-Me," because she looked like you so much!

But we all knew the one true love of your life was Nicholas. You loved him with all the heart a mother could muster up. He was your center. It makes me a little sad that he can't remember you as well as I can. It makes me sad that he was robbed of his mother when he was so young. I feel like he never really got to know you. He can never grasp that great love that you showered him with or just how much he meant to you.

The tragic events of that once obscure September day were so very hard to bear. The pain, the sadness, the emptiness. Mom and Dad were not the same people after that. Dad's eyes had a dullness to them. There was no sparkle . . . just existence. Though they were seemingly devoid of life, they continued to live. They tried their very best to be there for us—to be a source of support and strength. I am left wondering who provided *them* with support and strength? Who was there for *them* when they were trying so very hard to be there for us? I know that you were there. I could feel your presence and sense your aura.

You are my guardian angel and yet your passing taught us all a lot. I learned to trust God. I learned to slow down. I learned to live in "today" . . . for tomorrow is promised to no one. I learned to try to love even that which my weak human nature finds unlovable. I have learned to pray and to hope. I have learned to try to find the silver lining in everything—even in life's difficult and sad moments. I have tried to love others at the expense of myself . . . selflessly . . . just like you did.

Your memory will be with all of us forever.

Love,
Cindy

JOHN CANDELA

John Anthony Candela was born on February 23, 1959, in Newark, New Jersey, to John Cosmo and Phyllis Candela, and was the brother of Valerie, Karen, Joan and Joseph. He married Elizabeth Ann Davis in 1990 and had two children, Juliette Elizabeth and John Arthur. John earned an associate's degree in Business and worked for Cantor Fitzgerald. His entire world revolved around loving and caring for his wife and children. John also loved music, playing guitar, fishing, golfing and driving, with his family, in his thirty-fifth-anniversary Mustang convertible. On September 11, John was working as an OTC stock trader on the 104th floor of the North Tower. He was forty-two years old.

LETTER WRITER: Elizabeth A. Candela (wife)

AGE: 47

Dear John,
I changed the license plates on the Mustang to RADRLUV—just like that song, by Golden Earring. It's true, just like the song, you continue to show that your spirit and love for our family is still present . . . like "radar" love.

We've seen your signs. Joey spotted a hummingbird on 9/11. I was stunned by the appearance of this tiny bird, and I told Joey how much you loved hummingbirds. I knew it was a sign that you were safe, and that, even through death, you would never leave me.

I know how crazy you are about the number 3—like when we got married, you had to give me three wedding rings! And how on some days, at 3:33 p.m., you would call me from the trading floor just to tell me you loved me. You would say, as fast as you could, "I love you, I love you, I love you, I gotta go," and then hang up! It would always sweep me off my feet—the way you loved me was beautiful. Almost ten years after 9/11, we continue to see 3s, 33s and 333s. I know you hear us tell you, "We love you." Like the other day, when we were in the car on Juliette's birthday, Juliette and I saw 3:33 and shouted, "We love you." And just then, some song about a birthday came on the radio. Oh, John, that made Juliette so happy—it was a great birthday present. You would be so proud of her and Johnny. She has all of your musical talent. She has a beautiful singing voice, plays piano and guitar—in fact, I think she is actually better at playing guitar than you! And Johnny, he is looking more and more like you every day. He also has your silly sense of humor and desire to make people laugh. He still loves cars and cannot wait to be able to drive the Mustang! They both have your sense of compassion and generosity. And they both miss you so very, very much.

Thank you for all the signs. It never ceases to astound me how they continue to pop up, always in the most meaningful of situations—and always, when the longing gets too much.

I know you know, but we will never get tired of saying: We love you, we love you, we love you . . .

Beth

MICHAEL C. OPPERMAN

7₭

Michael Opperman was born on February 27, 1956, in New York, New York, to Jack and Ann Opperman, and was the younger brother of John, Joan and Carol. He married Debbie Youngblood in 1978 and had two children, Michael and Elisabeth. Michael worked for Aon. He was a devoted husband and provider for his family. He loved playing video games with his children and was an avid New York Mets fan. On September 11, Michael was at his desk on the 102nd floor of the South Tower speaking with his wife on the phone. He was forty-five years old.

LETTER WRITER: Carol Smee (sister)
AGE: 48

Dear Michael,

On September 11, 2001, you never had a chance. You assisted people on your floor to an emergency stairwell, and some are still alive because of you. You went back to your desk to call Debbie to let her know that you were okay. You were on the phone with her when the second plane hit. They never found your remains. You were on the 102nd floor of the South Tower.

My life changed forever as it did for my family. I definitely look at life differently. Live for today and hope for tomorrow. I am closer than ever with Debbie. God says things happen for a reason. I can't find a reason for this tragedy.

Not a day goes by that I don't think of you. I miss the phone calls and advice you always gave me. You always made me smile no matter what happened. My son J.P. took "Michael" as his confirmation name because he admired and loved you so much. Michael was married on July 9, 2011 (9/11), in honor of you.

I do not know why God takes the good ones. You will never be forgotten and I look forward to seeing you in heaven.

Miss you and love you, Michael.

Your loving sister,
Carol

KENNETH J. MARINO

~

Kenny Joseph Marino was born on July 9, 1961, in Brooklyn, New York, to Pat and Mary Ann Marino. He later moved to Oceanside, New York, and was very loyal to his favorite teams, the Mets, Rangers and Mariners. His real passion, however, was firefighting. Once he joined the New York City Fire Department, he liked to go where the action was, and moved his way up to Rescue 4 and then the elite NYC Rescue 1. He married Katrina in 1997 and had two children, Kristin, now thirteen, and Tyler, eleven. Kenny's company was in the first building that was hit, and the second to fall. His body was never recovered. Katrina has since been given Kenny's helmet and Halligan bar, which were recovered at Ground Zero. He was forty years old.

LETTER WRITER: Katrina Marino (wife)
AGE: 45

Dear Kenny,
I miss you. I miss everything about you.

When I sat down to write you this letter, I kept coming back to the last time I wrote you. It was October of 2001, about five weeks after we lost you. We held a memorial service for you and I lay awake at night wondering what to say. I wrote a poem to try and capture my feelings. Here is just a small part of it:

Kristin, Tyler and I were all lucky that morning,
If any luck could be had . . .
I happened to make it into the city early that morning,
And I thought it would be nice to surprise Daddy at the firehouse.
I saw the look of pride in Kenny's eyes as he put both children
In the driver's seat of "Daddy's fire truck"
And when it was time to leave,
We all got our kisses as Daddy went to each door of the car
And kissed each one of us.
I remember thinking what a special visit it was
As I drove away.
Little did I know when I saw that building collapse that day,
That our life as I knew it would never be the same . . .

Kenny, we miss you so much. You fit so much into your forty years, but it will never be enough. You are our hero, our angel, and will always be our special guide throughout our lives. We will always miss you, and we know that you are with us, and watching over us.

Love,
Katrina

ALAN DAVID FEINBERG

~𝕶

Alan David Feinberg was born on February 28, 1953, in Brooklyn, New York. He married Wendy Appel on March 26, 1978, and had two children, Tara and Michael. Alan joined the New York City Fire Department in 1981 and began his career working at Engine 40, Ladder 35 in Lincoln Center. In 1999, Alan became the Aide to the Fire Chief of Battalion 9, which was stationed in Times Square. When Alan was not busy fighting fires, he was always having fun, whether he was acting as "class dad," coaching soccer and baseball or taking care of his cars. He died saving others on September 11, 2001. He was forty-eight years old.

LETTER WRITER: Tara Feinberg (daughter)
AGE: 28

Dear Dad,

You had just packed me up and moved me to college at the University of Florida. I was a carefree eighteen-year-old with the world at my fingertips, and I was ready to explore each and every thing that life had to offer. Unfortunately, a week into my freshman year, that carefree attitude was lost to a new world full of grieving, loss, responsibilities and adulthood. I now had the choice—stay at school and experience all the opportunities that you and I had looked so forward to or give in, move home and be there for my mother and brother.

Well, I know what you would have done, and I made that choice for myself, too. I had to stay at school, life had to go on, and I wanted to live my life for myself because I knew it would have been what you wanted for me. And I can honestly say that we made the right choice. The four years I spent at the University of Florida were the most amazing years of my life. I made great friends, watched a lot of football, studied and learned so much about myself. Although I worried daily about Mom and Michael, I knew they would be okay without you or me there.

After college, I moved to New York City. I never thought I would want to live there, but I remembered how you always taught me that I was stronger than I thought and that I was capable of taking on any challenge or conquering any fear. I graduated from Hunter College with a master's degree in Speech-Language Pathology and now work full-time helping children on the autism spectrum.

You were always my hero for all the little things you did daily in our family, but on September 11, 2001, you became a hero to the world as one of the brave 343 firemen who gave their lives to help save so many others. I knew I always admired your strength, your compassion, your constant desire to help others and your dreams of making every day a better day no matter what, but on that day I truly understood what a selfless and remarkable man you were.

Even though it's been ten years, I still feel your presence. You are with me every day. You inspire me to live my life, to help others, and to be grateful for each moment. I don't know what the next ten years will bring in my life, but I do know that I have enough strength, wisdom and support to take on anything.

I love you always,
Tara

KENNETH W. BASNICKI

⇥

Kenneth William Basnicki was born on December 10, 1952, in Toronto, Canada, to William and Jean Basnicki, and was the older brother to Robert and Christopher. Ken married Maureen on December 8, 1984. Maureen's daughter, Erica, immediately loved her new dad and the family was soon joined by new baby Brennan. Ken earned an honors bachelor's degree in Business Administration at the University of Western Ontario in 1975. An avid skier and snowboarder, Ken had almost finished building the family's dream home near the ski hills of Collingwood, Ontario, where Ken also enjoyed mountain biking, golfing, beach volleyball and soccer with the kids. He had just been promoted as Financial Marketing Director for BEA. On September 11, Ken called his mother from the 106th floor of the North Tower. He was forty-eight years old.

LETTER WRITER: Maureen Basnicki (wife)
AGE: 59

Hi Honey!

I remember fondly when you were parked in our driveway at our home in Toronto. You called to say that you would be home in a half hour. When I reminded you that you were already there, you

said, "No, not yet!" You needed to make a business call on your cell. Once your work was done, you entered the front door and shouted, "Honey, I'm home!" And you made sure you weren't taking work home with you. Home time was family time with Erica and Brennan and me.

Your family was your top priority. Our son, Brennan, will always remember the call you made from Windows on the World, on the 106th floor of the WTC. The call was made on Sunday evening, September 9, 2001. At that moment, you were very excited, and told Brennan that you were on top of the world—on top of the world in life. You had been promoted in your business, but most important for you was that you were on top of the world with family.

Family was so important to you that you spent two years (your last two) building your dream home at Blue Mountain, Collingwood. This home was built so that our kids would want to come home. You hoped that they would ski or snowboard in the winter and mountain bike with you, play soccer or beach volleyball, which was something the family did each summer.

The landscapers were just putting the finishing touches on the backyard on September 11, 2001. You had gone to New York for a business meeting and to introduce yourself in your new position.

We all miss you, honey. And hope you are home!

Love you forever!
Maureen

STEVEN RUSSIN

٭

Steven Russin was born on June 7, 1969, in Bronx, New York, to Ed and Gloria Russin, and had a brother, Barry. Steven grew up in Marlboro, New Jersey, and received his bachelor's degree in Finance from Ithaca College, and immediately began working at Cantor Fitzgerald. Over the next ten years, he worked in various positions in the same department. Steven loved playing and watching a variety of sports, he had a great sense of humor and he loved children. Steven married Andrea on June 9, 1996, and had their first child, Alec, on September 22, 1999. Steven was a Vice President and a Trader for Cantor Fitzgerald. He was on the 104th floor of the North Tower. His twin daughters, Ariella and Olivia, were born four days later, on September 15, 2001. He was thirty-two years old.

LETTER WRITER: Ariella Russin (daughter)
AGE: 10

Daddy,

If Daddy was still alive
How different my life would be
We'd have lots of fun and family time

Lots of days we'd spend at the beach
Together we'd play lots of games
Life would really not be the same
I am always thinking of how much I love him
But I know he's always with me
And I am always with him

Love,
Ariella

Paul William Innella

🍃

Paul William Innella was born on November 11, 1967, in Brooklyn, New York, to Paul and Shirley Innella, and was the oldest of three, with siblings Maria and William following close behind. Paul earned his degree from Polytech Institute of New York and was employed by Cantor Fitzgerald as a Systems Analyst. Paul was an avid and excellent bowler, and also enjoyed golf, Fantasy Football, dancing, the Olympics, the band Kiss and all things Disney. He had a friendly and outgoing personality and always seemed to be the life of the party. Paul's daughter, Victoria Jacquelyn, was born on November 11, 1999, and she shares not only his birthday but his zest for life. On September 11, 2001, Paul was on the 103rd floor of the North Tower. He was thirty-three years old.

LETTER WRITER: Victoria Innella-Jones (daughter)
AGE: 11

Dear Dad,

Soon it will be your tenth anniversary in heaven. I just had my eleventh birthday on November 11. You know that, because November 11 was your birthday, too. I wish that we could celebrate our birthdays together and just forget about the anniversary.

I wish a lot of things. I wish that 9/11 had never happened. I wish that I had some memories of you. I wish that you could come to my dance recitals, and to my basketball games, and to my band concerts. When I see other parents there, it makes me miss you even more.

Mom says that you and I have a lot in common. She says we are both very friendly people who are the life of the party. She says we both love music (I even like Kiss, which I know was your favorite band), and we both love to dance. She also said that we both like to talk, talk, talk, and more than anything, we both love a good meal. Oh! Guess what else? I am a Mets fan, too. So, I guess I take after you in a lot of ways, even though for most of my life you have been gone.

I get to spend time with Grandma and Grandpa, Aunt Maria and Uncle Jim, Uncle Billy and Aunt Debbie, and Jimmy, Heather and Chris. Everyone misses you so much, and I always hear things about you when we are all together.

I think about you a lot, and I don't think that will ever change. I have a whole bunch of pictures of you—some people say I look like you, and some say I look like Mom. It's not fair that you are not here, and you didn't deserve what happened to you. It makes me angry and it makes me sad, too. Most of the time, though, I try to think about good things, and I am happy.

I know one day I will see you again. I hope you are able to see me now, so that at least it isn't like you are too far away.

I love you!

Love,
Tori

DAVID GARCIA

~🌿~

David Garcia was born on May 11, 1961, in Poughkeepsie, New York, to Stanley and Hiro Garcia, and was the brother of Richard. He married Deborah Rieb in 1987 and had two sons, Davin and Dylan. David earned a BS in Math and Computer Science from SUNY Cortland, where he met Deborah, and was working full-time as a Computer Programmer/Analyst and Private Contractor for Marsh & McLennan and part-time for GHI. He was passionate about his wife, children, extended family and friends, boating, skiing and music. He also had strong interests in self-improvement, securing a financial future for his family, finding a cure for retinitis pigmentosa and helping the Foundation Fighting Blindness. On September 11, 2001, David was on his way to his desk on the 97th floor of the North Tower. He was forty years old.

LETTER WRITER: Deborah Garcia (wife)
AGE: 47

Dear David,

I miss you. Not a day has gone by that I haven't wanted you to reappear in our lives.

Your boys are great. I'm so heartbroken for you that you've missed out on the joys of being their dad, shaping and watching them grow into men. Davin has his driver's license and loves music while Dylan is almost in high school!

I spent the greater part of the first five years after you left managing the circumstances of your loss, searching for you and juggling 9/11-related legal, financial and memorial tasks, raising and being available and healthy for the boys and your parents.

You are so amazing, how you've arranged to keep us taken care of even a decade after your leaving us here. You were always a good provider. Your dad is declining, perhaps you're aware. I'd say it began the day you left us. Your mom is strong, I just wish I could be of more help for them.

David, I married your brother and we now live with the boys in Vermont. I hope you don't mind, but I think you arranged it that way. It's a crazy, unpredictable life. Somehow I keep on going, like on a moving sidewalk, I pass through the days regardless if I deliberately step forward or not. But never without looking back. Some profess that you can't move on until you've closed the past. But there is no closure. I don't anticipate there will ever be. And nothing compares. There was no warning, no phone call, no letter, no body.

David, this is my "message in a bottle," a summation of my deepest sentiments. If I had the opportunity to express "final" words to you in this world (while holding you in my arms), I would say this:

Thank you for every wonderful day we shared together. You reside in the deepest parts of my soul and soon our souls and spirits will be reunited in heaven for all eternity. I know I will feel you smile down and embrace us when the seas rock our boat, your sons now at the helm, when the sun glistens on the mountain snows and when gentle breezes caress my skin. I love you forever . . .

Deborah X/O

LARRY JOHN SENKO

꤀

Larry John Senko was born on February 20, 1967, in Pittsburgh, Pennsylvania, to Ed and Margaret Senko, and had an older brother, Eddie. He grew up in Donora, Pennsylvania. He married Debbi Yusem in 1997 and had a son, Tyler. Larry earned a bachelor's degree from St. Francis University and worked as a Vice President for Alliance Consulting. He loved his family and friends, sports, driving fast cars and playing guitar to the Grateful Dead. On September 11, Larry was in a meeting in his office on the 102nd floor of the North Tower. He was thirty-four years old.

LETTER WRITER: Debbi Senko-Goldman (wife)
AGE: 45

Dear Larry,

Ten years ago began with despair, extreme grief and sadness. You were my first thought in the morning and my last thought at night. At the age of one, Tyler would kiss your picture and ask, "Why did Daddy go bye-bye? I wish he was here. I love him." Through my tears I would reply, "Daddy would be here if he could, and he loves you with all of his heart!" As time moved on, your memory is kept alive with beautiful and exciting stories about your extraordinary life.

A few years ago, I was lucky to find a man named Dan who fell in love with Tyler and me. I know in my heart that you sent him our way. He is a tremendous father and always respects your memory. Five years ago, we were blessed with a little girl named Lindsey. She is your namesake, and I am sure you are an angel for her. Our ten-year-old, Tyler, is so special. He is the ultimate sportsman, just as you were. He is an all-star baseball player and is exceptionally smart in school. He is polite and funny, and I hope he continues to have all the things you wanted for him. I love that I will always "see" you in him.

When the children ask questions about you, I always tell them how kind and generous you were. One of my favorite stories is that you always sent flowers to me at school when I was teaching. My coworkers would comment how sweet that was. Even sweeter was the day you sent a single rose to each lady in my wing so that they would not feel left out.

What I miss most is sharing our lives, our goals and our dreams. I also miss the special way we danced together and the way you held my hand. Our Grateful Dead collection continues to make me smile when I listen to it. I pledge to never let your memory fade.

I learned so much from you, Larry. You taught me how to love unconditionally and to have gratitude in my heart. I learned to try to focus on the positive when life gets tough and not to make the "little stuff" big. Dan and I will continue to pass on those values and teach Tyler to be the gentleman that you were.

Please watch over us. If you guide us, I know that we will make you proud. I will miss you and honor you all the days of my life. Thank you for loving me.

All of my love,
Debbi

Susan Leigh Blair

Susan Leigh Blair was born on May 24, 1966, in St. Louis, Missouri, to Sally T. White, and was the sister of Leslie. Sue grew up in Needham, Massachusetts, and earned her BA from Colby-Sawyer College and worked for Aon. She cherished her friends and family, but probably loved their children even more. Sue was happiest in the mountains or on the beaches of New England, with the sand between her toes, the wind in her hair and the sun on her face. On September 11, Sue was last seen shepherding her employees and her pregnant boss from the Aon offices on the 92nd floor of the South Tower. She never made it past the Sky Lobby. She was thirty-five years old.

LETTER WRITER: Leslie Blair (sister)
AGE: 47

Dear Sue,

On this tenth anniversary of September 11, Mara and Nicolas will stand with me in Lower Manhattan. We will wait to hear your name: Susan Leigh Blair. One name of 2,752. It is *our* name; you are *our* person. And this year, like all the previous years, I will wince when I hear it, and my heart will ache for all of the other families who are listening for *their* name, *their* person. Mara and Nicolas

Susan (left) and Leslie

have been with me and Mimi to mark other anniversaries—in Boston and in New York. They have stood by memorials with your name etched in granite. They have placed flowers on your grave. They have seen your beautiful face smiling at them from old photographs. They know the story, almost firsthand, of how the Twin Towers fell, and they know how I still cry because I miss my sister. But on this anniversary, I don't want to tell them the story of how you were killed. On this anniversary, I want to tell them just a few lessons that you taught me that I think they should know.

Lesson 1: When you know something is right, make a plan, persevere and don't quit regardless of obstacles or people telling you no. Like when you were just a baby and somehow managed to climb on top of the counter to grab some chocolate ice cream.

Lesson 2: Determination and perseverance are great, but have a backup plan. Like when the boys you used to throw crabapples at suddenly attacked back, you ran to me for cover.

Lesson 3: Regardless of your size, dress yourself well (and find a favorite brand that looks good on you). Impressions matter.

Lesson 3a: Be kind to people who help you, and don't be afraid to ask for what you want. You might get a promotion, or first dibs on the good stuff.

Lesson 4: Have at least two great friends who you respect and admire, whose company you enjoy and whose thoughts, hopes, dreams and despair you share.

Lesson 4a: Love for friends or anyone else should be selfless. You do for them because you love them, not because you are keeping score.

Lesson 5: Seek adventure, whether overseas or around the corner. Don't be afraid to try a new experience. I remember just how casually you could explore a new country with no agenda— just curiosity.

Lesson 6: Compassion, being interested, listening and understanding another person's perspective will enrich your life and the lives of others. You spent precious time with our grandmother in her last few months and enriched both of you in the process.

Lesson 7: There is incredible beauty in nature, so open your eyes. There is magic in the mundane, so open your mind. There is joy everywhere, so open your heart. When I think of you now, I remember your joyfulness, how you enjoyed hiking, the mountains, the oceans, sunsets, Lucy Kitty and driving around in that convertible with the sand in your toes, boots in the trunk, music turned up loud and your head thrown back in laughter. You were spontaneous, ready to make the ordinary special. You built a castle out of a big box with Mara. The kids ran through the sprinkler on a random Tuesday, and you signed Mara and Nicolas up for music lessons when they were just two.

In the days and weeks following 9/11, I had so many questions. But I was always certain that in your last moments, you never questioned that you were loved, and I never questioned that you loved us. And I think that might be the best lesson of all. We don't know how long our lives will be. But at the end, I hope we can say that we have lived with purpose, determination, bravery, adventure, compassion, friendship, joy and love, and that our loved ones are as certain of our love as we are of theirs. Surely, this is your legacy.

With love,
Leslie

PATRICK MURPHY

Patrick Sean Murphy was born on January 29, 1965, in Niscayuna, New York, to Thomas and Lori Murphy, and was the brother of Lori-Jean, Thomas and Timothy. He married Vera Profaci in 1991 and had two children, Sean Timothy and Margaret Jane. Patrick earned a BS from the University of Virginia and worked as a Vice President for Marsh & McLennan. He had a great sense of humor. Patrick loved his wife, children and family and had many great friends. Patrick next loved fishing on his boat *Nothin' But Net* and playing pickup basketball games in New York City and Millburn, New Jersey. On September 11, Patrick was at his desk on the 97th floor of the North Tower. He was thirty-six years old.

LETTER WRITER: Vera Murphy Trayner (wife)
AGE: 45

Dear Patrick,

I truly believe you know all of this, but so many ask me "What was it like?" and "How did you survive?" This is how I can describe it: On September 11, 2001, my life as I knew it crumbled with the World Trade Center towers. A frantic search ensued. A horror so awful had to be accepted. I saw myself on the edge of a cliff looking down into a void that was so dark and so deep and so wide. I was afraid to move for fear that I would fall into the abyss and never return.

I knew instinctively that I had to survive. Not for me but for Sean and Maggie. They were babies—just two and a half and four and a half years old. I was determined to build a life so that they could grow up in a normal way. They deserved it.

You and I worked so hard to create our life together I was never going to let it crumble to ashes. I came from embers of nothingness. This is where I started my journey. Then, I went into hyperdrive, filling out papers, applications, writing thank-you notes, keeping lists, making files. I worked until I could not work any longer. I worked through a veil of tears.

I tried to bring happiness to Sean and Maggie. We played, we cried. I received encouragement from so many people. I accepted help, I accepted kindness, I accepted love.

I began to feel a shred of normalcy. I returned to work. It took me two months to begin to feel the slightest bit productive. I balanced work, homemaking, parenting, the lawyers, the accountant, the financial planner, the paperwork, my family, your family, my friends and on and on . . .

With encouragement and love and the sight of Sean and Maggie being happy, the momentum continued. I felt success at work, my life began to be in order. I learned to have faith in myself, my determination and my creativity. It was an incredible journey to finally get across the abyss, but I am so proud to say I made it!

As the years move on, I am genuinely happy that Sean and Maggie are happy, well-adjusted kids who love to be with their friends, play sports and are doing well in school. The best compliment is when my friends and their teachers tell me how polite and caring they are.

Patrick, I am remarried now to a wonderful man, Andrew Trayner, whom I met in 2005. We live with the children in Tampa now. I am blessed to have found love twice in one lifetime. I never take anything for granted and I never sweat the small stuff in life. It's a good way to live and love.

I strive to do the right thing always, despite the path often being more difficult. I try to be generous in all that I do to show how appreciative I am that so many were charitable to me when I needed it most. My faith in God, and knowing I have the best guardian angel watching over me, keeps me calm.

Each anniversary of September 11, I still get so emotional and feel overwhelmed. There are so many ceremonies and vigils. I tend to go the opposite way and go to the beach, take our kids fishing or otherwise spend the day by ourselves. I am sick with sadness that you suffered in death and that you didn't deserve this fate. You were such a good guy who made a positive difference in the world, and we will never know how great your life could have been. I feel it is my duty to continue your legacy by raising the best children I can, continuing the scholarships in your memory and striving to be generous and kind whenever I see the opportunity.

I miss you and
will forever,
Vera

PETER T. MILANO

꿏

Peter T. Milano was born on August 10, 1958, in Brooklyn, New York, to Frank and Mary Milano, and had four siblings, Al, Frank, Tommy and Maureen. He was an avid Yankees fan and was renowned for being passionate in life, driven in work and commanded the room at any party. He honed all of these skills at the State University of Brockport, where he received his degree in 1980. His marriage to his wife, Patty, was exemplary for his son, Peter, and his daughter, Jessica. He was the epitome of a family man, his life revolving around their every activity, from Peter's basketball tournaments to Jessica's dance recitals. Professionally, he was the first Vice President of his Cantor Fitzgerald office on the 104th floor of the North Tower. He was forty-three years old.

LETTER WRITER: Jessica Milano (daughter)
AGE: 23

Dear Dad,
I am sitting on my couch in Brookline, Massachusetts, attempting to distract myself online with email, Facebook, and any other method of procrastination I can think of before buckling down to work. I open up my email account and notice that I have a new message from an address and name that I do not recognize. It is

not a forwarded email and does not appear to be any type of junk mail. The email turned a trip to Ireland from a beautiful memory into a sign from heaven.

Looking back, I am in the seventh grade, and we are on a two-week whirlwind tour of Ireland with you, Pete and Mom, celebrating Nan's seventieth birthday. During the trip, although we spent the majority of time with Nan's family, we did take the time to go to Gola Island, a part of Donegal, where your Irish family had lived for many generations. At first there was nothing particularly interesting about the island. My twelve-year-old self was bored, kicking rocks and avoiding the strangely abundant goose droppings that seemed to cover every inch of the gravel and dirt ground. It was at this moment of boredom, with my eyes glued on the ground, that you came up behind me and whispered, "Look up, Jessy. Look at the view." It was breathtaking. We stood on the edge of a cliff looking at a giant H-shaped rock cliff, watching the waters crash elegantly beneath. You and I instantly saw beauty in this natural wonder, and without speaking a word, we simultaneously decided to attempt to climb down.

If you remember, we didn't get very far before Mom found us and, not being quite as adventurous in spirit as us, she could not see why we would be so eager to climb down the potentially dangerous slope. I never felt anything but utter safety climbing with you beside me; but Mom insisted we *slowly* climb back up. When we reached the top again, you pulled out your ever-present camera and snapped a picture of the stunning vision before us.

We shared a special bond that afternoon. Although I am unsure why, we were both drawn so strongly to this spot, as if nature herself had created it for us to enjoy together. Less than a year later, we lost you.

Unbeknownst to me, you were not a stranger to that magical spot. You had been there before, years earlier, and fallen in love with its beauty. You had taken me to the spot so many years later to share in its power with me, your only daughter. On our first trip there, you told one of your cousins how much you loved that spot with the astounding view of the coast of Gweedore. Without knowing that we had shared a special moment at the edge of that cliff, your cousin and his family, the Sweeneys, built a memorial to your life at the exact spot we stood together.

Back on my couch in Brookline, I opened the mysterious email to discover that the beauty of that spot caught the attention of another man, simply traveling through Ireland, named Paul Burns. Upon seeing the memorial, and without knowing you or our family, he was moved to email me to tell me of its existence so many years after your passing, and attached a picture of the memorial that took my breath away. It was the exact picture we had taken ten years earlier, except where you stood, there was now a memorial in your remembrance.

Love,
Jessy

José O. Calderón-Olmedo

❦

José Orlando Calderón-Olmedo was born on August 27, 1957, in Fajardo, Puerto Rico, to Saturnino Calderón and Petra Olmedo, and was the brother of Elizabeth. He attended the Inter American University in San Juan, Puerto Rico, where he earned a bachelor's degree in Accounting. He enlisted in the U.S. Army on July 8, 1992, and during his second tour in Germany he met and married Gloria Garcia. He was then deployed to the Persian Gulf in support of Desert Storm. They had two children, Vanessa, nineteen, and José Jr., thirteen. He loved playing baseball and salsa music. José died in the Pentagon, where he was SFC Chief of Personnel. He will be remembered for his smile and his heart by his friends and family. He was forty-four years old.

LETTER WRITER: José Orlando
Calderón-Olmedo Jr. (son)
AGE: 13

Dear Daddy,
Always and forever
I wish you were here so
I can play basketball
With you and say thanks
For everything that
You did for us.
                    Love, José

Joseph Mathai

🖋

Joseph Mathai (aka Minoo) was born on March 27, 1952, in Kerala, India, to Dr. Chacko and Aleyamma Mathai, and was the fourth of five sons, Jacob, John, KK and Cherian. He married Teresa Louzado in 1989 and had two children, Michelle and Robert. After earning his Engineering degree from India, he came to the United States and earned an MBA from Columbia University. He worked many years on Wall Street before moving to Boston where he was Managing Partner at Cambridge Technology Partners. He loved his family, and his children were his pride and joy. He was an avid reader and he loved to jog. On September 11, he was attending a risk management conference at Windows on the World in the North Tower. He was forty-nine years old.

LETTER WRITER: **Teresa Mathai (wife)**
AGE: **38**

My Dear Joseph:

On that fateful Tuesday morning, I was on my drive home from carpooling the kids to school. The radio informed us that a plane had crashed into the WTC. I was worried about you; I knew you were at a conference in New York and that much chaos would ensue. I wanted to call you to warn you, but I did not want to dis-

turb you in the middle of your conference. When I came home and put on the TV, I decided to call you anyway, and reached you on your cell phone at exactly 11 minutes past 9 a.m. Mine was the only call that got through to you that day.

You told me your conference was at Windows on the World on the 107th floor of the North Tower and that a plane had just struck the building. I did not want to worry you by mentioning the second plane that had hit the South Tower, soon after the first. In silence, we both realized that this was something bigger than just another unfortunate airline accident.

You told me the air was thick with white smoke, and it was getting difficult to breathe, and that evacuation plans were being announced over the PA system. I told you to call your office to tell them you were safe, then we would talk again. At this point, there was a pregnant pause. I realized, you wanted to tell me you loved me, but you hesitated. You have always been the strong one in our family. You did not want me to think that you feared for your life, that you were not sure of the outcome; you did not want me to worry.

I told you I'd pray for your safety. I wanted to tell you that I loved you, but I bit my lip. I did not want you to think that this would be the last time we spoke to each other, that this would be our last chance to say goodbye, our last words.

As soon as I put down the phone, I changed my mind. Why wait? I tried to call you back, but the phone was busy. I tried again and again . . . but it kept going to your voicemail. I kept hitting redial . . . then I stared, transfixed with horror, as the North Tower imploded and crumbled like something surreal out of an epic disaster movie.

That day, I never got my chance to tell you I loved you. We all loved you! We never got to say goodbye. All these years later, we still miss you, and we will always love you, though those words went unspoken on that fateful day.

I have since mentioned that moment to our kids, now young adults. I told them, "Life is precious and life can be short. If you love someone, if you appreciate someone, take a moment to tell them what they mean to you. Take a moment to thank them. Tell them you love them. Several times a day, if need be."

And that is just what we do to this day.

With all our love . . . till we meet again . . . on the other side of the rainbow.

Yours,
Teresa

JASON CHRISTOPHER DEFAZIO

~

Jason Christopher DeFazio was born on July 12, 1972, in Staten Island, New York, to James and Roseanne DeFazio, and was the brother of Michael. He married Michele Moss in June 2001. Jason attended classes at the College of Staten Island. He worked for Cantor Fitzgerald as a bond broker, but was in the process of becoming a NYC fireman. Jason loved his family and friends. He was very athletic and played football, softball and boxed. He loved the New York Giants and the Yankees. On September 11, Jason was at his desk on the 104th floor of the North Tower. He was twenty-nine years old.

LETTER WRITER: Michele Pizzo (wife)
AGE: 35

Dear Jay,

September 11, 2001, was the worst day of my life. I remember you leaving in the morning, kissing me goodbye twice and saying, "I love you." Then seeing the horror of that day unfold on TV just a couple of hours later, not believing what was happening and never hearing from or seeing you again.

It is hard to remember a lot from those first couple of days because everything was such a blur. I remember waiting for you on the steps, praying that you would come home. I remember not eating for days because if I could survive without food, you could, too. I believed for weeks that you were alive somewhere but had amnesia. I don't remember exactly when I really believed that you were gone. It may have been when I was at one of the countless meetings that were held for all families. Finally a priest convinced me to eat because he knew that you would want me to be okay. I think at that moment I knew you weren't coming home.

With the help of family and friends, I started a memorial fund in your memory. We give out scholarships to students from your high school to go to college. I feel that you would be happy to help others achieve their goals. We have a fund-raiser every year, which brings all of our family and friends together to celebrate your life. I also started to run, which I never did before you passed. Since there were so many memorial races for those who passed on 9/11, I felt you couldn't be left out, so I ran these races with a picture of you on my back. I even ran the NYC marathon!

I went back to school and received my master's in Exercise Psychology, and started to work as a fitness specialist. I felt this was a good opportunity to begin a new life for myself. Ironically, the job was in the World Financial Center overlooking where the Twin Towers once stood. At first, this was hard for me, but then I started to have a sense that you were with me every day, helping me learn to live this new life.

Eventually, little by little, I began to move forward. About three and a half years ago, I met a wonderful man, Anthony. He is caring, hardworking and devoted. I really feel that you had a part in having me find him. He is so understanding and respectful when it comes to anything about you or September 11. He loves your family like they are his own. On November 6, 2010, we had our first child. I am excited to start this new life with him. I never could have imagined that after losing you I would be so happy again.

There is not a day that goes by that I don't think about you and miss you. I will always honor and remember you for the rest of my life. Thank you for letting me be a part of yours and for being "my special angel."

Love always,
Michele

John Anthony Spataro

꽃

John Anthony Spataro was born on March 16, 1969, to Giovanni and Domenica Spataro, and was the eldest brother of Robert and Anthony. After residing together in Mineola, New York, for six years, he married Patricia Wellington on July 8, 2000. John graduated from St. John's University in 1991 with a bachelor's degree in Finance and worked for Marsh & McLennan in their Working Capital Group. He adored his wife and loved his family and friends. He enjoyed writing, keeping abreast of the local and national political scene, and was also an avid New York Mets fan. On September 11, John was at work on the 98th floor of the North Tower. He was thirty-two years old.

LETTER WRITER: Patricia Wellington (wife)
AGE: 52

Dear John, My Love, My Best Friend,
Almost ten years have passed since I was last able to touch you or have you twirl my hair, and even though I speak to you every day and kiss your portrait that hangs in my bedroom, my heart still aches for *you*.

After losing you, the first few years were very hard, but the first year was unbearable. I believe the only thing that saved me was the puppy. I had stopped working and rarely got out of bed, but one day I had to go to the mall to buy a birthday present, and there happened to be a pet store as soon as I entered. I thought seeing the puppies would cheer me up a little, so I went in. There was this one little puppy that didn't move or go to the window like the other puppies; she just stayed curled up in a ball. The salesperson explained that she had crate depression because she had been at the pet store for four months. I asked to see her, and when he handed her to me she  grabbed onto my shoulder and would not let go. I took her home that day and I named her using your initials: JAS. It turned out to be a miracle, because we wound up saving each other; did you have something to do with that? I saved her from a crate at a pet store, and she saved me from wallowing in my grief.

How I miss our conversations about our future, our friends, politics and life in general. I especially miss your sense of humor. It was always there, even though most people missed it. You were very circumspect and quiet, but you were such a devoted and loving partner to me and a great friend to everyone who took the time to get to know you.

I've tried to make you proud of me, especially in dealing fairly with your family. It was very difficult and heart wrenching, but I returned my engagement ring to them. I thought it was the right thing to do since we were not blessed with our own children and since it was a family heirloom. Its rightful place is with your family.

There is someone else that I want to tell you about. I met a man not too long after losing you. Everyone talked me into accepting a date—I think just to get me out of the house. We went out on one date, but it was too soon for me. We lost contact, then after five years I ran into him again, and we started to see each other. He's a New York fireman who also lost a number of close friends and colleagues. We recently celebrated our one-year wedding anniversary. I know you would have wanted me to be with someone who would take care of me, so that I would not be alone, and it took me a long time to find someone who I respected, loved and trusted as much as you.

This in no way takes away from my love for you. Not a day goes by that I don't think about you or reminisce about times we had together. You will always be a part of me and always remain in my heart. Please continue to watch over us. And if you can, every once in a while please send me a sign to let me know you are still here with me and soon enough we will be together again. Our life here on earth is but a flash in time, but our afterlife together will last an eternity.

With my
never-ending love,
Your Tita

SARAH KHAN

～

Sumintra Budram (aka Sarah Khan) was born on August 24, 1964, in Zeelugt EBE, Guyana, to Thakoor and Sybil Budram, and was the sister of Kanhai, Angad, Danpaul and Surujapttie. She married Nazam Khan on July 31, 1988, and had two children, Shaneeza and Ameeza. She attended Zeeburg Secondary School. She loved her two girls and husband very much, and enjoyed traveling. On September 11, she was working on the 101st floor of the South Tower. She was thirty-one years old.

LETTER WRITER: Sybil Budram (mother)
AGE: 62

Dear Sarah,

I was so blessed to have such a precious daughter—one of character. Your smile and love won the hearts of many, including your three brothers and sister, and we were one very happy family when you were alive.

After you moved with your husband and kids to New York, you still came to visit us in Guyana every August. It was just eleven days after you returned from a visit that you lost your life. The attacks changed my life as a mother, and the lives of all who loved you. I had lost Dad just eleven months before that day, and then I had to suffer losing you.

I left Guyana to be with your two wonderful children in New York. I could not handle the sadness of your death; it was simply too much. Being in your home without you was difficult. Then, a very kind and loving person came into my life and helped me try to live and handle this great loss. The past ten years have been hard. I always keep looking to see you walking out on the street. Maybe, maybe, you made it out somehow. But I never do see you.

The memories of you I carry with me in my heart every minute of every day, and they sometimes bring tears to my eyes; sometimes they bring a smile. But the memories make me stronger and more empowered to be there for your two daughters, who love me so very much. As their grandmother, I know they are my future.

I love you, my dear, and miss you.

Mom

Mark Shulman

༓

Mark Shulman was born on March 27, 1954, in Brooklyn, New York, to Ira and Evelyn Shulman, and was the brother of Larry. He married Lori Zryb in 1977 and had two daughters, Melissa and Jamie. Mark earned a Mechanical Engineering degree from Pratt Institute and worked as a Fire Protection Engineer for Marsh & McLennan. He loved his family; taking vacations to Disney World; rooting for the New York Giants, Mets and Rangers; playing golf and coaching his daughters' soccer teams. On September 11, Mark was working on the 100th floor of the North Tower. He was forty-seven years old.

LETTER WRITER: Melissa Shulman (daughter)
AGE: 27

Dear Daddy,

I can't believe it's been ten years since 9/11. Sometimes I feel like you're just going to walk through the front door and share some hilarious work stories over dinner, or I'll find you sitting on the couch screaming at the Giants on television.

When I think about the last ten years, though, what sticks out in my mind are the moments when "your girls" have missed you most acutely.

All of the graduations—mine from high school (you would've loved my speech), college and graduate school, and Jamie's from high school and her upcoming one from college (she's doing so well and you can tell she loves what she's majoring in).

Jamie's Bat Mitzvah, only two months after 9/11.

Every Passover when we get to the "Let Us Eat!" part of the Seder, because no one can say it the way you used to.

In 2006, when Endy Chavez made that catch in Game 7 of the NLCS at Shea Stadium and I thought the Mets were going to win it all.

When Grandpa Ira died and I knew you would've been the perfect person to truly describe him.

Seeing my friends dance with their fathers at their weddings.

A few weeks ago, when Mark proposed to me. You would absolutely love him—he spells his name the right way, he roots for all of the right New York sports teams (he's even gotten me into watching the Knicks!) and he's an engineer. What else could you ask for! We're getting married November 5.

I could probably think of a million more moments, some big, life-changing ones, and other small, everyday occurrences, when I wished that you were around to offer your opinion, bounce ideas off of, chastise me and just talk to.

I know that you already know, but Mom, Jamie and I think of you every single day. You have impacted our lives so profoundly that we could never forget you. Ten years out, time has helped heal our hearts some, but it will never diminish how much we love you and how thankful we are to have had the time that we did together. Thank you for teaching me to "live life to the fullest," to "always have a sense a humor about life" and "to pull down your pants and slide on the ice." If I hadn't been your daughter, I never would have become the person I am today.

Missing you
now and forever,
Melissa

DENNIS CAREY

🍂

Dennis M. Carey was born on May 23, 1950, in Brooklyn, New York, to Joseph and Grace Carey, and was the brother of Ken, Desiree and Joseph. He married Jean Accardi in 1973 and had two children, Nicole Theresa and Dennis Jr. He was a firefighter and then trained in Special Operations, Hazmat 1. He loved his family, friends, cooking, traveling and animals. On September 11, Dennis was at the FDNY medical center for his yearly physical. He left to respond to the scene, and he was found in the stairwell of the North Tower. He was fifty-one years old.

LETTER WRITER: Jean Carey (wife)
AGE: 57

Dear Dennis,

You were taken from us doing what you did best—helping others—as you were on that treacherous day in September.

You cared for me, for our children, your extended family and friends. Since you passed, we have two beautiful grandchildren, Grace and Ryann. They would have been the best part of your life and you would have been the best grandfather. You were the kind of father that took part in every aspect of our children's lives. I will tell Grace and Ryann how you painted Halloween faces on their parents, and how you pressed and mended their clothes with the same enthusiasm you had preparing for vacations or camping trips.

I can only imagine the love in your smiling blue eyes as you watched them grow. I am sure that your grandchildren will have your dauntless ambition and desire for adventure. Grace loves to climb and explore everywhere her legs will take her. Ryann's smiling face and wide blue eyes personify your optimism, and we will watch the little one grow and see in her heart the strength of you.

You cannot be here to see their beautiful faces or hear their heartwarming giggles. And you will miss the arrival of our third grandchild. But you can be, and are always, a part of your grandchildren's essence that cannot be taken away. Your intelligence, benevolence, courage and endless sense of humor will be a part of all of us.

Heroism is the legacy that belongs to you.

Love,
Jean

JOSEPH P. MCDONALD

🦋

Joseph P. McDonald was born on March 11, 1958, in Brentwood, New York, to Joseph and Mary McDonald, and was the oldest of seven children. A natural athlete, he excelled at many sports and was even scouted for Major League baseball in high school; however, he instead chose to attend Carleton College and eventually became a broker for Cantor Fitzgerald. In 1988, he married his wife, Denise, with whom he had two children, Kathleen and Brigid. On September 11, he was at work on the 105th floor of the North Tower. He was forty-three years old.

LETTER WRITER: Brigid McDonald (daughter)
AGE: 17

Dear Dad,

You're no less present in my life now than you were the day I lost you. The smallest and most common things remind me of you. Every time I can't find something, I remember the tried-and-true advice you gave me one afternoon. I lost a necklace, so I asked you to help me search for it. Instead, you told me to look for a paintbrush in my room because you said I'd find what I wanted if I was looking for something else. I knew I'd never find a paintbrush in my room, but I tried your technique and sure enough, I found my

necklace. I look for paintbrushes quite often now and think of you each time.

My last real memory of you was the day before second grade started, just a few days before September 11. Nervous about school, I asked you what second grade was like for you. You reminded me that you had skipped the second grade, but you told me that I'd be fine. You were always a genius in my mind, and I wanted to be just like you. At the end of first grade, I remember your reaction when I found out that I had passed the test for my school's gifted and talented program. You were so proud of me, and that was just the best feeling. From then on, everything I did was to make you proud. It still is.

One of the most notable parts of our relationship was the way we bonded over music. My aunts and uncles still laugh at me because I was a Johnny Cash–singing five-year-old. But I proudly take that as a compliment because you bought me my first Johnny

Cash CD and taught me to love all the music you loved. My favorite song was one of your favorites as well: "Highwayman" by Johnny Cash, Waylon Jennings, Kris Kristofferson and Willie Nelson. This song holds a special place in my heart because it tells the stories of four characters who have died but who are "still alive" and "will always be around." They assure us that they will return to earth in some form, even if it's as small as "a single drop of rain." Their legacies live on long past their deaths, just as yours will.

You're part of a special group of people in history whose deaths represent the devastating effects of hatred. None of you will ever be forgotten, and you're all living through your descendants' memories. I sincerely believe that the world is learning from September 11 and will slowly but surely make peace. I just wish you could have lived to see it.

Love forever and ever,
Brigid